796.522 KIN
Kingery, Hugh E.
The Colorado mountain club

Colorado Mountain Club

The First Seventy-Five Years
of a Highly Individual Corporation

1912 - 1987

Evolution of the Seal

*On March 25, 1915, the Board adopted as the CMC seal the
"full front view of a mountain sheep's head,"
designed by Miss Hillier.
The club membership ratified this on April 23, 1915,
and approved spruce green and snow white as official club colors.
Somehow the bighorn
turned its face one-quarter sideways in 1916,
and all the way to the side in 1917 — its current outlook.*

The Colorado Mountain Club
The First Seventy-Five Years of a Highly Individual Corporation
1912 - 1987

By Hugh E. Kingery
Assisted by Elinor Eppich Kingery

Published in Cooperation with
The Colorado Mountain Club Foundation

CORDILLERA PRESS, INC.
Publishers in the Rockies

Copyright 1988 by The Colorado Mountain Club Foundation.
All rights reserved. No part of this publication may be reproduced, stored in a retrieval system, or transmitted, in any form or by any means, electronic, photocopying, or otherwise, without prior written permission of the publisher.

Library of Congress Cataloging-in-Publication Data
Kingery, Hugh E.
   The Colorado Mountain Club : the first seventy-five years of a highly individual corporation, 1912-1987 / by Hugh E. Kingery assisted by Elinor Eppich Kingery.
      p.   cm.
   "Published in cooperation with the Colorado Mountain Club Foundation."
   Includes index.
   ISBN 0-917895-25-8 : $8.95
   1. Colorado Mountain Club — History. I. Kingery, Elinor Eppich. II. Title.
GV199.8.C63K56   1988
796.5'22'060788 — dc 19   88-13932
                                                                                  CIP

First Edition

1 2 3 4 5 6 7 8 9

Printed in the United States of America.

EAGLE COUNTY PUBLIC LIBRARY
   BOX 240   328-7311
   EAGLE, COLORADO   81631

Front Cover Photograph
   Headed for the top — Mount Nimbus in the Never Summer Range. *Photo by Janet Robertson.*

Back Cover Photographs
   1913: Mount Hermon. *G.H. Heitz.*
   1917: New Year's weekend, Bear Creek Canyon. *Colorado Mountain Club Archives.*
   1920: Sunlight Peak, Needles Outing. *Colorado Mountain Club Archives.*
   1929: Arapaho Peak. *Everett Long.*
   1938: Pyramid Peak. *O.P. Settles.*
   1948: Mount Powell. *Louise Roloff.*
   1955: Mountain tent, Canadian Outing. *Louise Roloff.*
   1970: Eagles Nest Wilderness. *Hugh E. Kingery.*
   1987: Ski tour. *John Verbiscar.*

Cover Design
   Richard M. Kohen, Shadow Canyon Graphics

Design & Typography
   Shadow Canyon Graphics Evergreen, Colorado

Cordillera Press, Inc. Post Office Box 3699 Evergreen, Colorado 80439. (303) 670-3010.

Contents

Acknowledgments 7
The Colorado Mountain Club Foundation 9
Introduction 11
Foreword: *A Climb in 1906* 13
Chapter One: *To Unite the Energy* 21
Chapter Two: *To Collect and Disseminate Information* 51
Chapter Three: *To Stimulate the Public Interest* 65
Chapter Four: *To Encourage the Preservation* 71
Chapter Five: *To Render Accessible* 85
Epilogue 121
Special Articles from *Trail & Timberline* 123
Index 127

Gilpin Lake, Mount Zirkel Wilderness, August 1959. *Photo by Elwyn Arps.*

> These are the things I prize
> And hold of the dearest worth;
> Light of the sapphire skies,
> Peace of the silent hills,
> Shelter of the forest,
> Comforts of the grass,
> Music of birds, murmur of little rills,
> Shadows of clouds that swiftly pass,
> And after showers the smell of flowers
> And of good brown earth,
> And best of all, along the way
> Friendship and mirth.
>
> — Henry Van Dyke

Acknowledgments

We extend appreciation to many CMC people who contributed time, pictures, thoughts, and encouragement. We should especially mention the Group historians who provided us with their unfinished manuscripts of Group histories: Ann Hayes of the Boulder Group and Randy Jacobs and Jane Koerner of Pikes Peak.

Citations with the pictures and in the text mention others who have helped by providing both visual and verbal illustrations, both directly to us and in the pages of *Trail & Timberline* during its seventy-year career. Other special helpers included Sally Ross, Jan Robertson, and Urling Kingery.

We interviewed only a few; most information comes from the above sources and from the pages of *Trail & Timberline*.

Wham Ridge on Vestal Peak, 13,864 feet, looking east from Arrow Peak. *Photo from CMC Archives.*

The Colorado Mountain Club Foundation

The Colorado Mountain Club Foundation was created in 1973 to benefit the general public. It supports projects that relate to mountains, primarily those in Colorado, including research, books, films and lectures, access, trails, backcountry huts, conservation, education, and expeditions. For further information contact: The Colorado Mountain Club Foundation, 2530 West Alameda Avenue, Denver, Colorado 80219.

The generosity of the following individuals made this book possible:

Samuel Alfend
John Ambler
Harry and Selma Berman
Patricia Y. Berri
Andrews D. Black
Carl Blaurock
Mark and Margaret Bonomo
Whitney M. Borland
Polly Bouck
William and Louise Bradley
Henry Buchtel

Blake Clark &
    Rosemary Burbank
Sarah Burbank
Minerva Canavan
CMC Denver Group
    (Downhillers)
Carla S. Coleman
Gudrun Gaskill
Eleanor M. Gehres
Sam Guyton
Jean Franck

Vaughn Ham
Jean F. Hollister
O. L. Hough
Bob & Kay Hubbard
William J. Kunzman
William C. Leipold
Walter Livezey
Makalu Expedition
  (Glenn Porzak)
Karen Miller
Chuck and Judy Nichols,
  Nichols Expeditions
Ken Nolan

Irene Paproski
Ardis Rohwer
David Rosendale
Mr. and Mrs. Werner
  Schnackenberg
Ella Jane and Jean Settles
Dudley T. Smith
Joy Swift
Giles Toll
Frieda Uebele
Anne Vickery
Don Winner

CMC climbers on the summit of Mount Richtofen, 12,940 feet, 1914 summer outing. *Photo from CMC Archives.*

Introduction

Seventy-five years ago, did the founders of the Colorado Mountain Club envision a 7,500-member group with chapters in fifteen Colorado cities, several hundred trips in summer and winter, and activities as diverse as square dancing, technical ice climbing, and lawsuits to protect the environment? Did they expect our horizons to have expanded from Colorado to every continent?

Probably not, no more than we today can imagine how the Club will operate seventy-five years from now, in the year 2062.

Those founders did, however, have vision. They expected to take legions of people into the mountains, to help neophytes become mountain people who learned about and loved the high country. They expected to influence our governments to protect the mountains. They planned to let people know about these mountains which they loved.

Our organizational statement — written in 1912 — expresses these goals succinctly.

> We are organized
>   to unite the energy, interest, and knowledge of the students, explorers, and lovers of the mountains of Colorado;
>   to collect and disseminate information regarding the Rocky Mountains in behalf of science, literature, art and recreation;
>   to stimulate the public interest in our mountain areas;
>   to encourage the preservation of forests, flowers, fauna, and natural scenery; and
>   to render readily accessible the alpine attractions of this region.

How did our founders, and their successors, carry out these goals? This account tracks the Club's progress according to that statement.

Climbers on the way up Wilson Peak, 14,107 feet, San Miguel Range, 1931 summer outing. *Photo by H.L. Standley from CMC Archives.*

Foreword

From Trail & Timberline, August 1929, by George C. Barnard

Early in the summer of 1906 I received from Dr. Will P. Smedley, a cordial invitation to change a proposed climbing trio into a quartette. Their objective was to be the ascent of Uncompahgre Peak in the San Juan mountains of southwestern Colorado. My acceptance was immediate and enthusiastic. Since early boyhood I had waited for the opportunity to climb a real mountain. My mother's story of her ascent of Pike's Peak in 1865 awakened my first desire for mountain climbing.

Late July found us prepared (or should I say unprepared?) for our first San Juan trip. Dr. (Rev.) David Utter was the official and genial head of our expedition. He had tramped and climbed in many states, had visited the Indians of the lower Colorado River, knew much of the habits of wild animals and had learned the art of traveling light. He was a storehouse of general information, and many an hour about the evening campfire was enlivened by the quiet but interesting recitals of his previous exploits. Will Smedley had already climbed Longs Peak, and so was out of the novice class. His brother Clyde, fresh from a year's experience on an Arizona cattle ranch, was the other intrepid member of our party.

We held one preliminary meeting. Dr. Utter submitted the "grub" list he and Will had prepared. We figured a few minutes on the amount of funds required, scanned a small scale map of Colorado which showed Uncompahgre Peak in the Lake City-Ouray district and, without any very accurate information, decided that our walking trip should begin at Silverton. I had to be assured and reassured that bacon, cornmeal, sugar, flour, baking powder and salt would furnish a satisfactory diet for two weeks of strenuous labor. I was partially convinced, never more than partially. Knives, spoons, cups and small frying pans (one of each for each) and two handaxes comprised our camp equipment. Our commissary was faithfully quartered and each portion wrapped in a double blanket, which constituted one's bed and packroll. One long strap attached to each end of the roll, with enough of a loop for the arms to go through, the weight thus falling across the shoulders and back of the neck, was the means of carrying used by the others, while I invented a not altogether bad harness of webbing which, after some adjustment, proved less tiring on long marches. We had about twenty-six pounds in each roll, including necessary changes of underclothing and hose. We wore the then customary hob-nailed high boots, hard to remove and hard to get into when wet, and unnecessarily heavy at all times.

It is only fair to say that there was no organization or group in Denver twenty-three years ago prepared to disseminate reliable information on outing and tramping equipment, or on suitable food for such a trip, and people in general were not familiar with government quadrangle maps, many of which were then available. The idea of a light waterproof covering for our packs received no consideration, nor did we realize the great advantage of a light sleeping bag as against heavy woolen blankets. Our clothing was cotton khaki, with woolen shirts and heavy hose. If I remember correctly, we suffered to some extent from blistered feet, something that seldom occurs among Mountain Club members now.

In due season we stepped off the train at Silverton, spent the night in a rooming house, and tried, without success, to glean some definite information about the country surrounding our mountain. Inspection of our treasury showed that we could perhaps afford to take the Silverton and Northern narrow gauge train to Red Mountain and thus save several miles and some thousands of feet in elevation enroute to Ouray. At Red Mountain we took to our feet, and how we enjoyed those twelve scenic miles along the old stage road. We had been advised to leave our packs at the mouth of Poughkeepsie Gulch and retrace our steps from Ouray to that point and make camp for the night.

In Ouray I was told of the presence of many wild animals, including bear, in the upper Cimarron country. Consequently, I increased my burden by renting a Winchester 30-30, feeling that it would be a shame to have to pass up legitimate big game.

A couple of miles up Poughkeepsie Gulch we picked up an old mine

Equipment of the 1920s: George Barnard had well-worn hobnail boots, Polly Bouck sported smooth soles, and Elinor Kingery's hobnails were attached to calf-length boots. *Photo by H. M. Kingery.*

trail and followed it virtually to the summit of Engineer Mountain, descending without difficulty the comparatively gentle, grassy slopes, on the north side, which extend east and north to the American Flats. Here at the head of the north fork of Henson Creek we spent a moist night, after a drenching day. I believe it is still safe to recommend

American Flats to anyone who wants a sample of a verdant and wet, above-timberline park. Leaving camp on Henson Creek, we rapidly approached our objective. Uncompahgre lay almost to the north, outstanding among the many fine peaks which surrounded us. Court House Mountain [Coxcomb?] and Wetterhorn were names unknown to us then, but both rose majestic on the western skyline as we traveled north. We ate our lunch that noon at an elevation something over 12,000 feet and, still following the contour, found ourselves at the base of the south ridge of Wetterhorn about 2:30 in the afternoon.

It was evident to everyone that we were passing a peak that was worthy of our metal [sic], both in difficulty and in height, but no one of us had heard of another 14,000 foot peak in that immediate vicinity. Finally Will Smedley, gazing upwards, said, "It would be a shame to leave that handsome bump behind." We all agreed. So, leaving our packs on the crown of the rust colored south ridge, we started and I found myself climbing my first real mountain.

The ascent was not difficult, but the route was not obvious; each one chose his own way. The views were superb, and our usual afternoon thunderstorm was gathering. Soon I had my first thrill of looking over a precipice, doubled back and tried a different route, then on to a ledge, wondering where it would end, then scrambling up between spires, only to be shut off by another cliff, but always up and up. Suddenly I realized that the others were out of sight and hearing, whether above or below me I had no definite notion. One thing was obvious: The way to the top was definitely up, and I kept on. The air grew colder, big, angry clouds were coming in my direction, there was an unusual tingle in the air. I did not understand it then. Suddenly I found myself above the minor spires among which I had climbed, and realized that I was approaching the real summit. The only apparent way to proceed was along a ledge some four feet wide, forming almost a trail, and partly circling the final spire. Realizing that a 600-foot drop was below me, I went on to this shelf with a feeling half exhilaration and half fear. Again I felt the tingle in the air, and suddenly I had the unmistakable sensation of my hair rising. Breathless, I wondered whether fear would really raise one's hair. If I had known static then as I do now, I would have guessed that something besides fear was influencing the locks beneath my hat.

Presently I came to a place on the ledge where the spire was apparently disintegrating and slide rock extended a short steep distance up toward

Wetterhorn Peak, 14,017 feet. *Photo by H.L. Standley.*

the vault of heaven. I stopped, called to my associates and, fearing to remain longer, scrambled up over loose rock for a hundred feet and found myself on the summit of my mountain. The roll of thunder, the blackness of the clouds and the tremendous depths on every side gave me a very insecure feeling. I called to my friends and, getting no answer, decided to sit down and hold on if I could find anything to hold on to. In a few minutes I heard voices and soon the others joined me.

It required very little time to explore the summit of Wetterhorn. There was no evidence of anyone else ever having been on top of the peak. No suggestion of a cairn — not even one stone on another. The clouds shut in from the west, cutting off our view. We decided that wisdom called for a hurried descent, yet not too hurried. As we left the summit, Dr. Will remarked, "Awful scary, George, awful scary," to which Dr. Utter replied, "Not scary at all; just be sure of every handhold and every foothold." As he spoke, letting himself down on the slide rock, a boulder the size of his head slipped from under his foot, bounced two or three times and then dropped off into six hundred feet of misty atmosphere. Will looked at me and we smiled, a sickly grin. There were no further words. We had suspicions that with an avalanche of rock we might bounce over the shelf like the first stone. Soon we were on firmer footing and half an hour later were back on our rusty iron ridge, where we picked up our packs, just as lightning began crashing

Wetterhorn Peak, 14,017 feet. *Photo from CMC Archives.*

all about us. Another sage remark from Dr. Utter, "Boys, at a time like this it is a wise thing to walk about a hundred yards apart, so if one is killed there will be someone left to carry him out." We separated and the lightning crashed.

Fifteen terrifying minutes and the storm had passed. All four were still alive. With our packs on our backs we headed due east towards the base of Uncompahgre. Coming to a boulder field perhaps a mile in extent — there was a difference of opinion. Dr. Utter took to the high ground on the left, the Smedleys a hundred yards to the east of him, while I picked a course across the boulders still farther east. Suffice it to say that we all arrived at the same point on the other side of the boulder field within thirty minutes.

An abandoned miner's cabin at an elevation of about 12,500 feet was there waiting for tenants. We were soaked to the skin and more rain was coming. Dr. Utter hated to have a roof over him, but timberline was three miles down the Cimarron. "Here is where we stay," he said, and there we stayed, sleeping on a board floor, the hardest ever laid. We burned everything available during the night in an attempt to keep warm. Finally daybreak came. Bacon and corn cake brought our spirits up to par, and we proceeded to climb Uncompahgre, our original objective.

Again we ascended via a south ridge, over an excellent government trail which brought us to the summit of Uncompahgre in less than three hours. We dropped rocks off the precipice on the north face, and estimated a thousand feet before they struck. Dr. Utter stood and looked over unconcernedly, while we three dug our toes in and lay on our stomachs as we looked over, confiding in each other that our venerable leader had lived a long time anyway and could afford to take some chances that we could not.

Descending Uncompahgre was easy. We took to one of the first rock slides which run up high on the west side of the south ridge. Taking hold of hands, we plunged down through this at a great rate, descending to our camp in short order, and here we began our long and wet but picturesque and enjoyable trip down the Cimarron to the Gunnison. And so ended our first San Juan trip, one that we can never forget.

Northeast face of Uncompahgre Peak, 14,309 feet. *Photo by Paul Gorham.*

Chapter One

"To unite the energy, interest and knowledge of the students, explorers and lovers of the mountains of Colorado . . ."

"There is a highly individual corporation in Colorado which has been doing an increasing business now for ten years," reported Denverite Lucretia Vaile in April 1922. "It was incorporated for the public service and assumed certain obligations toward the state . . . to make the best of Colorado's most striking resource — its mountains.

"Possibly it sounds a little presumptuous for any company to organize for the systematizing and distribution of God's blessings — which certainly seems to be the thought in these statements — and some citizen peer may wish to know how the founder of the Colorado Mountain Club got his appointment to such a job.

"Well, he volunteered. Not only did he volunteer but he started a custom of volunteering, and ever since the founding of the club it has been the habit of its active members to see and be glad in the wonders of out-doors and to try to multiply that pleasure by division with other people. And there is this to be said in extenuation of the club's presumption: the club is not a close corporation. Shares can be bought. The price even in these expensive days [of 1922] is only $4.00, a good reputation, and an interest in the out-doors. Contrary to a rather common impression, not even a vigorous physique is required. If the would-be stock-holder be lame or halt but can either hear or see, the club has something for him, for its dividends (paid every little while) come in the shapes of addresses and illustrated lectures as well as walks. There is not preferred stock; it is all common and capable of infinite increase without depreciation. The more share-holding nature-lovers there are in this corporation the better its business and the larger the returns to the individual."

Volunteers: Boulder Group chairmen assembled for Boulder's fiftieth anniversary. Front row, kneeling: Franz Mohling, Bill Herzer, Damon Phinney, Baker Armstrong. Back row: Everett Long, Ruth Wright, Ken Wright, Bob Kamper, Stan Boucher, George Dobbins. *Photo by Sue O'Brien.*

ORGANIZATION

The seven who assembled on April 3, 1912, came by invitation of Mary Sabin and James Grafton Rogers. Lucretia Vaile reported, "We talked about the desirability of such a club and the probable feasibility of it, and named over the mountain conquests represented by the group there present. It's my impression that we had, among us, climbed about sixteen peaks." (According to newspaper clippings in the Club scrapbooks, Mary Sabin had climbed seven of them — several with her sister, Florence.)

They scheduled a second meeting, on April 26, 1912, and twenty-five signed on as charter members. Two days later the Club held its first trip: to Cheesman Park Pavilion "under the guidance of Mr. [Ellsworth] Bethel for the purpose of making acquaintance with the Colorado mountains as seen from Denver.

"The first hike was on May 30, under the leadership of George

The CMC Charter.

James Grafton Rogers cuts the fiftieth birthday cake, April 5, 1962. *Photo by Jim McMillan.*

Mary Cronin, first woman to climb all the Fourteeners. *Photo from CMC Archives.*

Barnard, to the top of South Boulder Peak." The scrapbooks report that in that first year the Club conducted ten trips.

In the early days, Jim Rogers and Mary Sabin graciously credited each other with the inspiration to form a mountain club. Later, though, in reminiscences published in the Club's monthly magazine *Trail and Timberline* (*T&T* in the Club vernacular, and usually in this history), Mr. Rogers said the Club stemmed from a letter he addressed to the public which the "leading Denver newspaper," the *Denver Republican*, published August 1, 1911. Invited to the formative meeting were those who responded to his letter. In either event, Miss Sabin encouraged the organizers at the beginning. She attended the twentieth anniversary celebration; Jim Rogers cut the birthday cake at the fiftieth.

Membership has waxed and waned: 1,314 belonged in 1923, but the Depression took a severe toll. In 1934, only 416 belonged (that year Mary Cronin reported that the Club dropped sixty-eight people who hadn't paid dues for at least two years). By 1952, membership had started to revive, with 907 (646 in Denver; 64 in Pikes Peak). In 1960, there were 1,251 members; in 1970, 3,532 members; and by 1980, 6,329 members. Today the Club boasts 6,584 memberships; by adding kids and spouses included in family memberships (which the computers can't count), the Club has about 7,500 members.

Proud of its achievements over the years, the Club celebrated its fiftieth anniversary with zip. On August 18-19, 1962, CMC scheduled climbs of all the 14,000-foot peaks in Colorado. Abysmal weather caused several climbs to abort, so that climbers reached the tops of forty-seven out of the fifty-three Fourteeners. President Ken Wright commented, "We can be proud of the good judgment displayed by those who turned back, as well as the achievement of those who were successful." Statistics, interpolated from the report by Elwyn and Louisa Arps which they called, because of the dreary weather, "The Non-Shining Mountains": over 400 climbers climbed 115,400 feet to gain the forty-seven summits. The Mount Sherman climbers described the weekend: "sunshine, rain, snow, thunder, and lightning."

Roy Murchison at age eighty led thirty-one climbers up Grays and Torreys; twenty-eight Class A hikers (they usually hike the easier trails) went up Mount Evans from Summit Lake. Climbers on Little Bear lugged up a birthday cake, "although they found lighting fifty candles in the wind a bit difficult."

An anniversary convention in Estes Park brought workshops and

Climbing North Maroon Peak, 14,014 feet, Snowmass Wilderness circa 1938. Photo by O. P. Settles.

The Club's first trip went to Cheesman Park to view the mountains, as identified by Ellsworth Bethel. A copy of this photo, which was unearthed during the preparation of this history, has a note on the back in Jim Roger's handwriting that identified the event but not the people. *Photo by George Barnard from CMC Archives.*

seminars on mountain-going and mountain lore, and of course, hikes and climbs: 575 came to hear and to participate.

The Club had celebrated before: in 1932, all but one past president attended the twentieth birthday dinner. (Jim Rogers was out of town, but Mary Sabin came.) Speaker Henry Brooks, after recounting the first twenty years, concluded by saying, "Though the Mountain Club has grown and expanded, it has deviated little from the ideals and purposes of its founders." The same holds true today.

Volunteerism continues to run the Club, just as in CMC historian Lucretia Vaile's day. Sally Ross, a Club administrator, commented in 1985 that personal rewards motivate volunteers; the Club obviously motivates well, judging by the number who volunteer. Bud Saum, president in 1982, said, "You can't pick up an issue of a Group newsletter without reading at least one appeal for volunteers. Why such emphasis on volunteers? Because the Club runs on volunteers — that's why."

Another president reported, "I've been in the office during working hours and at times it has looked like a national emergency was in progress, with phones ringing, members checking out books, and visitors wanting personalized service." In 1949, the office handled 33,000 pieces of mail, 6,000 telephone calls, 2,000 visitors, and 3,155 registrations for trips. With today's Club three times as big, the volume of those activities has increased commensurately.

* * *

We modern folk think we have started new activities, but the founders really began most of the programs which we have now — although by sheer size we today have expanded the programs into more and grander things.

Take, for example, the trails: Municipal money built the Beaver Brook Trail west of Denver about 1917, "but," reports Miss Vaile, "it was suggested by CMC member Barnard, routed by CMC geographers, and obtained by CMC persistence."

Take, for example, another trail: The Fort Collins Group, working closely with the Forest Service and the CCC in the thirties, built the Mount McConnell Nature Trail, established registers on Greyrock, Bald Mountain, and other peaks.

Take, for example, legislative action affecting the mountains. In 1921,

The first hike, May 30, 1912, to South Boulder Peak. *Photo by George Harvey, Jr., from CMC Archives.*

To celebrate CMC's fiftieth anniversary, the Club, on August 19, 1962, scheduled climbs of all the 14,000-foot mountains in Colorado. Neil Wernette and Irene Paproski unfurled a homemade flag on top of Colorado's highest, Mount Elbert, 14,433 feet. *Photo by Virginia Nolan.*

the Club bore "an honorable part in the fight" to defeat a bill before Congress which threatened to permit grazing and irrigation in the national parks.

Take, for example, Junior groups. The students of Cheyenne Mountain High School, members of the precursor of the Pikes Peak Group, were granted a junior group membership in the CMC in 1919. They sound quite resourceful, for they bought a cabin which they permitted the Mountain Club directors to use for meetings!

THE GROUPS

This "highly individual corporation" has a highly individual structure of local "groups." Each sets its own dues, added to the state dues. The Juniors aim for minimal expenses, the Denver Group has an office to run, and Boulder and Fort Collins back the Club's conservation efforts with an extra five dollars tacked onto the regular fee. Boulder and

Denver, as well as the state organization, each send representatives to the statewide coalition of environmental action organizations.

The first groups to affiliate with CMC already existed as hiking clubs (Pikes Peak and Boulder). Later groups mostly formed from scratch, like Fort Collins and the Denver Juniors. All groups share the Club philosophy, summarized by early Boulder Group historian Gladys Curtis as "the right use and enjoyment of the mountains."

Denver — The Denver Group did not even exist as such until 1938. In *T&T* most early references to the "CMC" meant what we now regard as the Denver Group.

At its formal birth in 1937, with Elwyn Arps as first chairman, Denver members composed two-thirds of the Club. This proportion, more or less, persists today, and with this huge clientele, Denver faces associated

The second of the rainy suppers on the May 29-31, 1915 overnight to Craig Creek. *Photo by Charles Price from CMC Archives.*

Louisa and Elwyn Arps on the 1960 Needles Outing. *Photo by Louise Roloff.*

problems. The Denver Group chairman has the biggest responsibility in the Club, and the biggest job. Denver's diverse program, its status as an employer of an office staff, and, simply, its size, demand of the chairman executive qualities.

People and times changed. "In the early days," said Cedric Kaub in 1962, reviewing the Club's first half-century, "mountaineering knowledge was limited to the relatively few members who acted as leaders, and transportation was much more difficult to arrange. This meant less independent climbing and made the Club more necessary. The membership during the early years was more permanent and stayed with the Club for longer periods than is the case today when we have a turnover of about 200 members each year."

Either because of size or turnover, by 1947 not everyone knew everyone else — and therefore everyone else's climbing skills. To address this, Denver initiated a classification system of people and of trips. In 1947, trips were "easy, moderate, and difficult." In 1950, they became Classes 1-4 plus Technical. The classification scheme has undergone a series of changes and now consists of Classes A-E plus Technical, plus eight categories for Ski Touring. The system now applies to both trips and people. Most other groups have adopted the trip classification system, but not the people classification, which they leave to the judgment of leader and member.

The Denver system was not the Club's first, however. In the early days members could become "Qualified" members by climbing a 14,000-foot peak. Originally they paid extra dues for this recognition

— three dollars instead of two dollars — but by 1922 everyone paid the same — four dollars. Although this feature of Qualified Members received little attention after the first two decades, the Club did not eliminate it from the bylaws until 1953, when, said Cedric Kaub, chairing a bylaws revision committee, "Climbing one 14,000-foot peak is no longer an achievement."

Council members dickered over things like interest sections, trip fees, classification systems, and, particularly, finances. From a 1958 State Board meeting came the report, "All groups are active and in good condition, except that Denver is somewhat concerned over financial matters."

By 1953, demand for membership grew and Denver inaugurated orientation meetings for new members. Eventually attending one of these meetings became a prerequisite to membership.

Growth also expanded the types of trips. From time to time Denver has had sections concerned with backpacking, ski touring, downhill skiing, snowshoeing, bicycling, photography, square dancing, bridge, and other social activities. Now the Group newsletter supplements the

Early Pikes Peak Group officers and climbers on Sentinel Point. Top to bottom, then left to right, Dr. Edward Jackson, Eleanor Bartlett, Hubert Strang; Eleanor Davis, M. Davis, Harry Standley; Pearl Turner. *Photo by H.L. Standley from CMC Archives.*

The first of the annual Pikes Peak Group Wild Flower shows in 1920 displayed over 200 species of wildflowers in vases donated by Van Briggle Pottery. Here, the organizing committee at the 1950 show: Margaret Floyd, Jim Turner, Sara E. Wilks, Dr. Floyd Penland, Julia Wagner. *Photo from CMC Archives.*

summer and winter schedules by announcing monthly a plethora of special events, hikes, lectures, social events, and requests for volunteers.

Pikes Peak — The Cheyenne Mountaineers, a handful of students at Cheyenne School, led by Lloyd Shaw, formed the precursor of the CMC's first group outside Denver, the Pikes Peak Group. *T&T* described Shaw as "a young man of vision and determination, [who] has a knowledge of the outdoor sciences coupled with a great zeal for mountaineering which makes us wish we could use him in two cities at once." After affiliation with the CMC in 1919, reported Mary Shirer, "Nothing seemed too hard to tackle — trail marking, nature trail building, protection of birds and wildflowers, keeping picnic and campsites clean and helping to prevent forest fires by watching campfires."

People joined primarily for the hiking. Year after year they explored canyons like Williams, Waldo, and Bear Creek; local mountains like Baldy (Almagre), Garfield, and Herman. They reached trailheads by trolley and train. Group historians Randy Jacobs and Jane Koerner say, "Though poor roads and a lack of private cars kept them close to home, they ventured on occasion into the Tarryalls, and by 1924 two trips to the Sawatch . . . appeared in the schedule."

Pikes Peak sponsored, for twenty years, a wildflower exhibit for three days every July. Initiated by Pansy Green and William Penland, it informed both residents and tourists about Colorado wildflowers and their preservation. At the Public Library and the Chamber of Commerce they also maintained display boards of conifers which grow in the area.

Replacing the specimens as old ones became dry required a great deal of attention. These conifer displays proved so impressive that during World War II, libraries at Camp Carson and Peterson Field asked the Club for similar exhibits.

Hard times hit the Group in the thirties, say Jacobs and Koerner. "At 7:30 in the evening January 17, 1936, the Pikes Peak Group of the Colorado Mountain Club convened at the YWCA Building to vote on withdrawing from affiliation with the state organization and forming the Pikes Peak Mountain Club. This drastic action was precipitated by the steady decline of membership (to forty-three) and the unwillingness of the parent organization to reduce dues. It was reasoned that a local hiking club could operate on a leaner budget, thus encouraging membership with a lower annual fee. After much discussion on both sides of the question, Mary Shirer [moved that the Group] remain part of the state organization for a one-year trial period during which a determined effort [would be made] at improving the attendance at Club functions by the addition of such activities as swimming, lectures, dancing, and news bulletins published from time to time. The motion passed with a margin of one vote."

The Pikes Peak reporter to *T&T* did not mention this dramatic event, but rather continued to report on Group hikes as usual.

However, Group treasurer A. G. Ellis reported in 1939 that the Group discontinued its bank account due to the expense of "maintaining small checking accounts; accordingly, the Treasurer has kept the funds with his personal deposit. This procedure increases the responsibility of the Treasurer and proportionately decreases the security of the Group. For this year at least the change has been justified in that it has lessened Group expenses and the Treasurer has up to the present firmly resisted the temptation to abscond."

The crisis passed, and the Group remains a vital member of the CMC, now with over 500 members. They still hike the local canyons and climb the local mountains, and they still take excursions to the Sawatch and other high ranges.

Boulder — Respectful and deferential words mark the contemporary descriptions of the 1920 enfoldment of the Front Range Club into the CMC as the Boulder Group. In June 1920, *T&T* welcomed "forty hardy, wholesome, experienced mountaineers of the little city at the foot of the Flatirons . . . who can cook in the rain, sleep on the rocks, tramp without ceasing, and smile through it all; whose ideals are high, and whose traditions shine beside those of any mountain club in the land."

The Front Rangers acknowledged as leader "Pop" Thompson, a/k/a Frank E., Professor of Education and Anthropology at the University of Colorado. He sounds like a remarkable man. Ann Hayes (1988 Boulder Group historian) reports, "He milked his cow twice daily, and refused to own an auto. He liked to boast that he slept best out under the open sky tucked between two logs with a slicker on top." His fellows included a substantial contingent from the university, and in fact Jan Robertson (1971 Boulder historian) declared, "The real business of the Club in the early years was conducting the University's summer

Pop Thompson leading group, trudging on foot but with sleeping bags and snowshoes. Included in picture from front to back: Pop Thompson, unknown person, Florence Kendall, Claribel Kendall, Helen Murch, Robert Burns, C. Henry Smith, Daphne Smith, Gladys Curtis, Doris Stratton, Georgia Snow, Peg Thompson, unknown person, Hopkins, Harry Curtis. *Photo from Boulder CMC Archives.*

Recreation Department." In 1921, she reports 166 picnickers, ensconced in touring cars, attended an all-day excursion, 145 people "went and were fed fully" on a Wednesday evening outing to Bluebell Canyon, and on a three-day trip, 130 of 160 made it to the top of the Arapaho Peaks.

This Arapaho trip became an annual tradition, with the aforementioned supply of climbers typical. It continued: in 1950, 275 including cooks and guides headed for Arapaho Glacier. "Practically everyone who started up was able to reach the saddle. About twenty-six were led onto the glacier itself . . . loads of excellent food, no casualties except a slight sprained ankle, and a few cases of altitude sickness."

By 1980, Boulder had grown to 1,000 members and like Denver did not know the abilities of all. To clarify Club policies, a Safety and Leadership Committee issued a comprehensive *Leader Manual*, which explained general outings policies and policies for specific types of trips. In 1987, the council endorsed a set of leader qualifications. The Group has no formal course, but holds seminars for leaders.

The 1923 Arapaho Glacier trip, Hugh M. Kingery at left end, Severance Burrage at right end. Those in-between are unidentified. *Photo courtesy of Elinor Kingery.*

Juniors rehearse for the follies on top of Grays Peak. Jeannie, Your Friend and Mine, Downrock Q. Stumblefoot, Sigy, C.A. Kidd, Ruggie, and Arghness Sigh Yawn. (Also known as Jean Settles, unknown, Dave Bucknam, Susie Campbell, Susie Hurlbutt [Bucknam], John Wolcott.) *Photo from CMC Archives.*

Boulder's postwar activities have included the usual hikes and climbs, plus many activities centered on its cabins. Half of Boulder's 1987 summer schedule trips were rock climbs sponsored by the Group's Mountaineering School. That speaks to the allure of the Flatirons and their compatriots.

Each group has a character of its own; Boulder's has always stemmed around camaraderie and bon vivantry, the Brainard Lake cabin (and other cabins), and associated activities, rock climbing inspired by the city's Flatirons backdrop, and CMC's strongest conservation voices.

Denver Juniors — Unique among the groups, the Denver Juniors accept no members under age fourteen or over age twenty-one (technically; lots of Juniors hang onto their memberships until someone finds out they are too elderly). They began their mountain odyssey in 1930 with three official trips and representatives from each Denver high school. The first outing, ten days in the Cameron Pass area, cost participants $8.50 each.

The Nature Protection Group began sponsorship of the Juniors, but that emphasis on nature appreciation passed as the Juniors paid more attention to climbing activities.

As a separate group the Juniors have their own council elected each year and attain actual experience in leadership and mountaineering.

This also saves the "Seniors," i.e., the adults in the Denver Group, from, as Mary Hitch (Bowles) put it in 1949, "the fate of having wild young high school and college kids on their more normal trips."

Through most of its existence, the Juniors have had a special sponsor — their advocate from and to the Seniors: George Kelly, Malcolm Lindsey, Tad "Big Daddy" Frost, Bill "Mother" Davis, Dave Bucknam, and now Mike Berman. Junior rules require an adult sponsor on each trip (they eschew the term "chaperone"). One sponsor commented, "I believe that no one can be taught how to sponsor a Junior trip by reading about the various duties and responsibilities of a sponsor in T&T. The sponsor must know when to sit on the Juniors and when to let them run wild. Such knowledge is not learned out of books."

Periodically committees review the relationship and status of the Juniors, and each time reinforce the Juniors' unique situation: they are an independent CMC group, but with a special relationship to the Denver Group.

They attack mountains with a vigor much envied by older and less energetic Seniors, although they don't always end up on top. Only three topped Mount Elbert on a 1950 trip. "We were hindered by a strong wind which knocked more than one person over. . . . Excuses varied from the ones who were too far back and too slow to the girl who sat down to rest on South Elbert and fell asleep for an hour. And then there was another who slept on his side and had a sunburn line down the middle of his face." The April climb ended with a "wonderful thousand-foot glissade."

Junior emphasis changes, although food always seems important. A 1949 pie-eating contest on a Leadville street ended up with the girls smashing the pies into the boys' faces; the boys, after a successful chase, allowed the girls to share that pleasure. Some time in the 1960s they started carrying watermelons to the top of each summit. Juniors favor a stewpot concoction called "Grunge," actually a tasty mixture of hamburger meat and canned corn and tomatoes. And for a while, in order to foster Junior cuisine, various Juniors wrote a T&T column called the "Ptomaine Ptarmigan."

The Juniors had counterparts in Fountain, at Colorado College, in Boulder, in Fort Collins, and in Pueblo for short periods, but these small groups did not outlast their founders. The Denver Juniors have ups and downs as well; the seventy-fifth anniversary year found them rising again after a year or two of quiescence.

The first Western Slope Group climb (joint with Denver Group) ascended Mount Sopris in June 1950. *Photo by Bob Beverly.*

Western Slope — Midst a September 1949 snowstorm on Castle Peak, Harry Harris and Bob Beverly conceived the idea of a Western Slope Group, which came to fruition May 26, 1950, in Rifle. The first climb, a joint trip with the Denver Group, reached the top of Mount Sopris.

The leadership has a unique quality: all chairmen except one and many of the active members have been geologists, engineers, chemists, and persons associated with the field of energy development. Most worked in oil, coal, or oil shale. Accordingly, said Bob Beverly in *T&T* in 1981, "The Group's leadership may have a different and more development-oriented view toward certain conservation measures than may at times be expressed by the CMC Conservation Committee."

During the first two decades, the Western Slope Group centered its primary interest on high peak climbing, but the current, larger membership has much broader interests including cross-country skiing, desert and canyon country treks, bicycling, technical climbing schools, and local hikes. Bob comments, "Thirty years have slipped by since a small group of mountain lovers over on the other side of the Divide from Denver started climbing together under the flag of the Colorado Mountain Club. We are proud to be a part of the CMC and will continue to support its basic objectives."

Longs Peak — A combination of ardent outdoor enthusiasts and CMC members formed the Longmont group in May 1963. Their name

Climbers on the Narrows, Longs Peak, 14,256 feet. *Photo from CMC Archives.*

recognizes the dominant feature on Longmont's western skyline, and it became an unwritten law of the organization that each year the Group would sponsor and lead a climb of Longs Peak. By now they have shepherded several hundred people up their namesake. They extend an invitation to local residents who wish to participate, and therefore choose nontechnical routes.

Russ Palmer anchored the Group by serving almost continuously in one capacity or another on the Group council, and leading innumerable trips. Another member, journalist Lorena Darby, also served well the State of Colorado and our CMC principles in the Colorado State Senate.

The Group, said Lorena Darby in a 1976 *T&T* article, "by natural and physical selection, soon resolved itself into two entities: the 'reachers' (a/k/a 'eager beavers.') for the end of the trail or the summit of a mountain; the 'lookers' (a/k/a 'huffers and puffers') who paused often to be sure they didn't miss anything visible and appreciable en route. The eager beavers have gone on reaching those summits most of us will never know. The huffers and puffers have gone their way, too, not missing a thing. (Lest you think the latter group has scaled no heights, then consider Haystack Mountain, Rabbit Mountain, Twin Sisters, Steamboat Mountain, Coffintop, and other Front Range landmarks!)"

Huerfano Group — Like several other groups, the Huerfano one came to CMC already formed — as the Huerfano Outing Club. The Huerfano Outing Club started on "a cold, bleak day, November 6, 1932 . . . in the days when few thought of roughing it, climbing mountains, or being curious about fauna, flora, or the wide open spaces; days when jeans, shorts, and bandanas were yet to be dreamed of. . . . These were the days when one wore woolen tweed knickers, knee-length golf hose, high-top boots, long undies, a woolen shirt and sweater, headgear being a beret or a long-used felt hat."

Janet Chatin reports that on that first trip seven climbers, two of whom had attended CMC summer outings, faced "a howling wind lashing across the rocky ridge which marked the way to the summit" of East Spanish Peak.

Thirteen charter members joined CMC on November 11, 1935. The Group concentrated on hiking trips in the Walsenburg area; *T&T* accounts of their activities describe trips to the Spanish Peaks area, La Veta Pass, and the canyon country of the Purgatoire River. They followed Indian trails, found arrowheads and petroglyphs, and knew much of the human and archeological history of the area as well as the natural history. Sad to say, the Group disbanded in 1963, as the El Pueblo Group filled the southern Colorado niche.

El Pueblo — Organized in CMC's golden anniversary year (1962), El Pueblo has offered southern Colorado members a varied menu of trips. Their business is not always business; *T&T* reported that at the March 1964 regular business meeting, "business was at a minimum since [Dr. Yvonne Johnson] talked about the 1963 Peruvian (CMC) Expedition and showed some of her wonderful slides."

A 1964 trip climbed Mount Sherman "legally, gaining 3,000 feet" according to reporter and subsequent *T&T* editor Paul Stewart. Hikers to Badito Cone, said Bill Arnold of a 1967 trip, "tramped over pieces of rhyolite that looked and sounded like broken dinner plates." He reported on a 1966 trip by quoting Stan Boucher who was reporting

El Pueblo Group climbers on Eagle Peak, Sangre de Cristo Range. Anna Taussig, Paul Stewart, Freddy Carter, unknown person. *Photo by Dave Carter.*

on a 1947 Colorado College Junior climb of Quandary: "Nothing whatever happened on this trip. Everything went off smoothly. Climbers like to be on such trips, but it is difficult to talk about them afterwards."

San Juan — The San Juan Group has participated since 1965 as the most distant (from the Front Range, not from the San Juans), in that desirable part of the Colorado Rockies (to many from the Front Range). San Juan enjoys the freedom of a small group — members meet once each year to plan the entire trip schedule for the next summer and winter. They produce the typical mix of climbs and winter trips. The 1987 summer schedule took them on three trips in the San Juans, one in the Sawatch, and one in New Mexico (Wheeler Peak, the state's highest).

Aspen — Outings for this Group are "casual" and often "spontaneously organized," said Group chairman Gus Hallum in a 1973 interview. Aspen concentrates its trips, naturally, in the nearby Elk and Sawatch ranges. They have a close relationship with the Aspen Mountain Rescue Group. Fred Braun spearheaded in 1953 the organization of both groups as well as building five backcountry ski huts (which he still runs and which many CMCers appreciate). The citizens of Aspen appreciate Fred, too: the city held a Thank-you Day for him June 20, 1975.

Denver Wilderness Kids — Another unique group aims at families with young children. For Bill Hunter it started with an outing at the Sand Dunes National Monument over a Memorial Day weekend. "It was great . . . we were able to go back every year for the next four years as either leaders or followers.

"It seems that a group of kid-oriented people had put this Denver Wilderness Kids idea together back in 1974, thinking that there must be other families interested in getting their kids into the wilderness experience. It's been lots of fun helping to keep the idea going. Like helping a kid onto a rock for a giant's view or searching for just the right rock, the one that will skip almost two times. Digging a kid out of the snow, or into the snow. Balancing on a log, snowball fights in June. It's been fun being a kid!

"Well, it's 1987 . . . Eddy is fifteen years old now . . . eleven years of getting kids into that wilderness experience . . . and myself along with the kids. . . . I'd like to take that Sand Dunes trip one more time so, if you're not doing anything next Memorial Day, let me know. I'd

Five Wilderness Kids peek over the rock: Andrea and Nena Davis, Joey Nye, Eddy Hunter, Tara McLean, August 1979. *Photo by Bill Hunter.*

like to finish this Wilderness Kids experience the way it all got started . . . or maybe they might just let me be a guest leader in the future, sometimes I hate being an adult!"

Enos Mills — Estes Park supported a CMC group in the halcyon days of the twenties — from 1922 to 1925. The 1924 annual banquet drew forty-five to dinner (and a few more after dinner) to hear Robert Rockwell's "well-known and interesting illustrated lecture on 'The Birds of Colorado.'" But many members found summer too busy, and many left town in winter. The Group disbanded with an expression of continued interest in the Club and an offer of assistance to the winter outing and summer trips.

In 1976, as interest in Club activities expanded throughout the state, a new Estes Group formed with a new name. Thirty-five attended the first special program — a ski trip (by color slides) across Boulder-Grand Pass from Thunder Lake to Grand Lake. An active conservation program looked at timber cuts and litter removal. George and Wanda Cowles have served as mainstays of the Group.

Sky Pond and Taylor Peak, Rocky Mountain National Park. *Photo by Leonard Ellis.*

Glenwood — This Group self-started in 1983 in the canyon country — Utah's Grand Gulch. They offer a variety of outings, from day hikes to caves; desert sojourns to river trips.

West Elk, Weld County, Friends of Colorado — The Club continues to expand, within and without Colorado. CMC has new groups in Gunnison and Greeley, plus a generic out-of-state Group born in 1987 called Friends of Colorado.

The West Elk Group was born from and specializes in mountain bike tours for riders of all abilities. The 1987 schedule took them on five bike tours, two climbs, and a nature hike.

The Friends, coming to the CMC through trail building and outings, is not the first non-Colorado Group. Los Alamos, New Mexico, holds that distinction. The Los Alamos Mountaineers, an energetic bunch of high peak and technical climbers, affiliated with the CMC, from 1962 for ten years. For CMC's fiftieth anniversary, they contributed a climb of Culebra. This energetic group specialized in rock climbing and rugged peak climbs.

CLUB SECRETARIES

The secretaries of the Club have always had a special place and influence. Many Club members first meet the Club in the person of the secretary — although lately the secretary has multiplied from one person to four, plus several volunteers who answer the telephones at night.

Mary Sabin volunteered as first Club secretary after the first two meetings in the ballroom of Mrs. Junius F. Brown (in whose house she lived). George Harvey succeeded her and served until 1919. However, his principal contribution to the Club was not his secretaryship but rather his skill as a trip leader. Early CMCers regarded him as one of the best trip leaders the Club has ever known. "He was one of those stalwarts who were The Club." He also played the cello in the Denver Symphony and took fine photographs.

Katherine Bruderlin (Crisp) served as Club secretary from 1920 to 1922. She became one of Colorado's leading botanists and shared wildflower lore with anyone fortunate enough to travel with her on

Katherine Bruderlin (Crisp), Grace Harvey, and Agnes Vaille, here sporting stylish spectacles, each led the Club in the 1920s as climbers, administrators, and conservators. *Photo from CMC Archives.*

Club trips. She also headed the Club's Nature Protection Committee for years.

The success of the Club demanded a paid secretary: 1,000 members created enough of a demand that the Club hired Alice Manard for a year, and then Elinor Eppich, now Kingery. Hours — 9 a.m. to 1 p.m.; jobs — secretary, librarian, general information center; salary — fifty dollars per month.

Grace Harvey followed, for twelve years (1926 to 1937). She developed the job to the important place it now occupies. A devoted Club member, she went on all the outings and many of the day trips. They called her "the Grace note."

Evelyn Runnette served longest — 1937 to 1951. Just as active as Grace, she climbed the Fourteeners, knew the state, and went on outings. During the war years she pinch-hit in many other Club jobs and filled some new ones, like keeping outing ration stamps under control and solving problems arising from lack of transportation and gasoline.

Anne Byrd Kennon came next: a gracious, competent, self-effacing businesswoman. She never joined the Club, as she felt that a more independent status would help keep her out of the orbit of Club politics.

Her successor, Ella Jane Settles, had belonged to the Club for many years, had climbed with all the greats, was married to one of the Club's ace photographers (and herself past chairman of the photo section),

The "Grace Note." *From CMC Archives.*

Cedric Kaub (Club historian and 1935 to 1960 leader) and Evelyn Runnette (Club secretary) savor the top of Mount Powell, Gore Range, on a 1948 outing.
Photo from CMC Archives.

and has children still involved in the Club.

The next secretary had a different tie to the Club; Enda Kiley's father, famous writer and naturalist Enos Mills, had worked with early Club members to establish Rocky Mountain National Park.

Then came Sally Richards, an enthusiastic participant in the Club and its activities. As she served in the office she expressed her enthusiasm for Club activities with numerous articles in *Trail & Timberline*.

Marian Peterson came to the Club in 1972 as the first full-time secretary. Although she never attended a Club trip, her friendly way and her friendship with the Club and its members endeared her to all with whom she came in contact. She represented the Club to the public and to the members effectively. When the Denver Group recognized her dedication at an annual dinner she said, "I don't feel it's been an effort; it's been such fun."

Marilyn (no-relation) Peterson (now Micklick) stepped into Marian's shoes and has conducted the office with businesslike efficiency, a crucial asset to an organization grown to 7,000 members.

The Club has always enjoyed the right person in the important secretary's job, and the women (and man) who served us have had an important part in the development of the Colorado Mountain Club.

COLORADO MOUNTAIN CLUB FOUNDATION

Not a CMC group, not even part of the highly individual corporation, the CMC Foundation furthers the general aims and philosophy of the CMC for the benefit of the general public. The majority of its board members must belong to the CMC. In 1975, the two-year-old foundation had a fund of only $770; by 1988, its endowment alone exceeded $50,000. Though donations come mainly from CMC members, the Foundation mainly supports projects that benefit the public: various trails, including many miles of the Colorado Trail; climbing expeditions to the world's high peaks such as Makalu and Yalung Kang; conservation; Rocky Mountain Rescue Group; outdoor education programs for grade schoolers; college fellowships for research in the Colorado mountains (on subjects like acid rain, rare plants, and the bighorn sheep of the Club seal); and backcountry hut projects, including a photovoltaic system at the Brainard cabin. (Jan Robertson commented regarding the electric lights [which replaced candles] fueled by this modernism, "Some people think the lights are spooky but I think it means the cabin won't burn down.")

In addition, the foundation has assumed a lead role in publishing books on the Colorado mountains: *Summmits To Reach*, Mike Foster's annotated edition of Franklin Rhoda's 1874 journal of the Hayden Survey, *Heading and Distance Charts for the Colorado Fourteeners*, by Alan Silverstein and Barbara Euser, and this history of the highly individual CMC.

CLUBROOMS

CMC has had a clubroom office since about 1920. The Club has resided in a series of rented offices, from the public library to the Mining Exchange Building. Finally, in 1974, the Club became a property owner. Taking out a $55,000 mortgage, it purchased an old church which it turned into a real CMC home. Eleven members advanced the money and became mortgagees. Due to the efforts of many, the Club paid off the mortgage eight months early, in 1979. Flea markets, anonymous donors, a members' $55 club, *inter alia*, raised the capital to retire this first major Club debt.

The facility has served the Club well. It houses the paid staff, the Club library, meeting places, archives, and has an auditorium for regular programs. Hit-or-miss landscaping became formal with a 1982 refurbishing. Nighttime at the clubrooms sees people and committees scrambling for space to conduct Club schools, lectures, and committee meetings.

The clubrooms on West Alameda. *Sketch by Jerry Albright.*

Dear mrs. MAYFIELD

—ROCKY MOUNTAIN NEWS—32
Tuesday, July 13, 1948

She Lost Him to the Mountain Club

DEAR MRS. MAYFIELD:
I have lost my husband to the Colorado Mountain Club. I put up quite a fight—but I lost.

I had the old fashioned notion that children needed the moral and spiritual training of a father as well as a mother. I had a notion that the father should devote week-ends and Sundays to his children. But I was wrong.

On week-ends and Sundays my husband had to take part in mountain club activities. He had no time for us at home. As a result I bitterly opposed his Mountain Club contacts—and my husband in turn bitterly opposed me.

So, we got a divorce. That's the long and short of it. If I had named a corespondent in the suit I would have named the Colorado Mountain Club. This club just as surely stole my husband from me as though it had been "the other woman" in the case.

Well, Mountain Club, you can have him! But he'll regret it! Will you supply him with love and care for him when he becomes an invalid, or visit him if he has a complete mental breakdown and spends his declining years in a hospital?

Will you support him when he loses a job? Will you furnish him with the joys of sons and daughters, and a raft of grandchildren to gladden his heart? Will you, I ask?

Well that's it, Mrs. Mayfield. I am now a sadly
DISILLUSIONED MOTHER.

DEAR DISILLUSIONED:
What a sad mistake you made in coming out so openly against your rival! What a different story might be told if you'd handled things more tactfully.

Oh, I'm not meaning to blame you. You've suffered enough. But I am saying that you were at fault in letting a mere organization break up your home. If it had been another woman, well, that's different.

I had a letter from a woman the other day saying she was losing her husband to golf. Still another wrote that her husband spent so much time at the Elks Club that he might as well be married to it. I know a man who spends every available moment fishing and his wife quite frankly says he loves a trout stream more than he does her. So you see others cope with similar problems.

But the fact that a man has strong interests outside his family needn't lead to the divorce court.

* * *

YOUR MISTAKE was in being unwilling to share your husband. If you had been more tolerant of his Mountain Club activities, you might have worked out a compromise. But your forthright opposition set up an antagonistic current between you. You made him more stubborn than was natural. And more defiant.

Your very opposition made the club assume proportions of importance far out of scale.

All of which, I suppose is water under the dam now. Or is it? Could it be possible that looking back and recognizing your mistake might lead toward a reconciliation? Might make him realize how wrong he was to neglect his family in such a gross degree? People sometimes re-marry, you know. M. M.

* * *

An aside from Club publications: Frankie Foster, wife of the editor of the *Rocky Mountain News,* faithfully attended outings in the forties and fifties. In the *News* she wrote a column, a local and early Ann Landers type. One wonders whether she wrote both the letter and the answer to Disillusioned Mother.

Chapter Two

"To collect and disseminate information regarding the Rocky Mountains in behalf of science, literature, art and recreation

Trail & Timberline, the Club's primary vehicle to disseminate information on the Rockies, celebrates its seventieth year in 1988. The faithful publication of this magazine not only has carried out the purpose expressed above, but also has served to facilitate the unity of Club members, by providing reliable communication and a remarkable chronicle of Club and mountain events.

The Club's first publication was not *Trail & Timberline*, but rather a series of pamphlets on the wildlife of the mountains. Today they seem like puny discussions of the obvious — but in 1915 glossy color field guides for bird, mammal, and flower identification did not exist.

In the twenties, the Boulder Group, with the help of the Boulder Chamber of Commerce, published *Mountain Wildlife of Northern Colorado* and in 1932 produced *A Guide to the Geology of the Boulder Region* by Dean P. G. Worcester, professor of geology at the university. They revised it in 1950. Fort Collins put out a circular on *Wildflowers of Northern Colorado* in 1933, designed for elementary schools and friends of the Club. They posted it at the beginning of the Mount McConnell Nature Trail.

The most successful Club publication was, and is, the *Guide to the Colorado Mountains,* edited by Bob Ormes, an energetic climber who taught English at Colorado College in Colorado Springs. The Club Publication Committee (Betsy Cowles Partridge, Carl Blaurock, and Henry Buchtel) persuaded Bob to edit the guidebook. Publisher Alan Swallow doubted the success of a climbing guidebook as a business venture, but finally agreed that if the CMC put up half the publication costs, he would put up the second half in the form of supplies and work. The Club's share was $1,000 — an anonymous CMC member

If Ormes had sent the climbers to the southeast instead of southwest, they might have enjoyed this view of El Diente from the top of Mount Wilson. Photo by H.L. Standley.

contributed this. Club member and Eastman Kodak employee Henry Staehle furnished eight color photographs by Club members for the book through a Kodak experimental color fund which he managed.

Despite Alan Swallow's doubts, the first edition of 1952 sold out. (In 1983, the eighth edition of the guidebook came out, with 5,000 copies printed.)

Ormes used Club trip reports and topographic maps to write the book — "editing" seems like a modest term for the amount of work involved. Some errors crept in, he admitted. "One Monday morning some climbers who had tried my route on Mt. Wilson pounded on the door to complain about a typo: The book directed them to go from the Silver Pick Mine to a pass on the southwest; it should have been southeast. They went southwest, in the rain, spent the night out, and did not appreciate the blooper. This was the first edition — a typo — and I hadn't even seen the book yet!"

"I put in a funny route on Huron, created by my observation while climbing Missouri. George Gibson, from Colorado Springs, said to me, 'You wrote that blasted book — what did you think you were doing with *that* route?' It turned out to be full of downed logs and tough problems; they did not get out until well after dark."

On the other hand, Esther Holt reported that the Denver and Western Slope groups, on a joint trip, used the guide on a scheduled climb of Mount Elbert. "Bob Beverly led the ascent and made good use of our fellow-member's guide book. We believe that this is the first time that the 'Guide' has been taken along and referred to on a scheduled climb since it came from the press. Would that it were printed on 'engineer's' linen."

The bloopers were rare, the book a success.

The Club already had two mountaineering books under its belt: a gazeteer of all the named summits in the state with elevations, compiled by Roger Toll in 1923. The second, *Fourteen Thousand Feet*, combined the two subjects on which the Club's publications have centered — mountaineering and history. The first edition (1925) contained an account by Jerry Hart of the origin of the names of Colorado's forty-seven 14,000-foot peaks; the 1931 edition added a guide to routes on the Fourteeners, compiled by Elinor Kingery from Club records.

The 1931 edition also added four to the list of mountains with the magic 14,000-foot altitude. Since then surveys have periodically revised the list of Fourteeners. The list topped off at fifty-four during the boom time of the 1950s. The last revision subtracted Grizzly and Stewart and added Holy Cross, for a net total of fifty-three. *Trail & Timberline* carries an on-going discussion of the criteria which make a Fourteener; tradition seems to prevail over consistency.

Through the years the Club has published revisions of the guide to the Fourteeners, and guides to hiking and climbing in various parts of the state. Boulder put out guides like the 1965 "Boulder Mountain Park Trail Map" and a more recent "Ski Trail Map" for the Brainard Lake and Middle St. Vrain areas (primary author, Harlan Barton).

The Club produced other unique publications. "Front Range Panorama" identified Denver's mountain skyline from City Park with an eighteen-foot outline sketched by Trudy Pierce and Edith Ward from photographs by Elwyn Arps, text by Louisa Ward Arps and map correlation by Orlando Ward. It was a new kind of mountain publication. The Longs Peak Group followed the idea with "Longmont's Mountain Skyline," by Aurel Morgan and Russ Palmer.

The masthead of *Trail & Timberline* uses a drawing of Mount Meeker and Longs Peak by an unknown artist.

In *High Country Names* the Club took another chance; this dictionary of the names in Rocky Mountain National Park contains lively prose and extensive, meticulous research by Louisa Arps and Elinor Kingery. It does more than discuss the names — it tells about the people, the wildlife, and the scenery which compose the park, that early conservation achievement of the CMC. The book has entered into a third printing, and letters continue to come in asking about sources the authors used.

Historical pamphlets included Percy Hagerman's notes on *Mountaineering in the Elk Mountains* and William Brewer's 1869 geological journal.

The Boulder Group published its history (first fifty years) in a lively book, *The Front Rangers,* written by Janet Robertson. It serves as a role model for this history.

Now the CMC Foundation has taken over the publishing function for the Club and chooses the subject matter using various criteria: interest to Club members (like this one) or contribution to mountain lore or technical knowledge (like Mike Foster's annotated Hayden Survey journal and a scholarly study of coal mining in western Colorado). It also sponsors brochures from the Club Safety Committee warning about the hazards of avalanches and lightning.

The principal legacy of the Club to mountain science, literature, art, and recreation, however, is *Trail & Timberline*. This remarkable magazine comprises a history of all of those subjects. Leafing through back issues of the magazine can entertain any Club member for hours. It contains an extensive history of the Club and its interests, from first ascents to flower walks, from foothills hikes to ski mountaineering, from columbine protection to wilderness preservation, from the Colorado Rockies to the highest Himalayas. The collection of T&T's offers an invaluable resource for anyone who wants to know what happened in the CMC or who wants an overview of Colorado's mountain recreation and conservation history.

T&T supplies most of the quotes contained in this history — and also supplies most of the historical information which we have compiled herein. It has carried significant articles such as the six-part series, Botanical Explorers of Colorado, accounts of first ascents in the Rockies, and authoritative articles on the high peaks and their elevations.

CMC has long had a fascination with mountain nomenclature, perhaps climaxed with *High Country Names*. Direct action started in 1914 when Harriett Vaille Bouck and Edna Hendrie persuaded three Arapaho Indians to go on a pack trip in what now is Rocky Mountain National Park to learn about Indian lore and names in the area. *Arapaho Names and Trails* by Oliver Toll printed the field notes (forty-eight years later).

Ellsworth Bethel, charter member, named the Indian Peaks — and in turn had a Clear Creek valley peak, once known as Clear Creek Pyramid, named for him. A 13,120-foot peak in the Sawatch, christened in 1958, honors Billy Kruetzer, first ranger for the U.S. Forest Service (appointed in 1898 to Gunnison National Forest and in 1921 to the Roosevelt National Forest) and honorary member of the Fort Collins Group. The Indian Peaks have Mount Toll, named in 1941 for Roger Toll, superintendent of Rocky Mountain National Park from 1921 to 1929 and of Yellowstone from 1929 to 1936, CMC charter member, and active CMC leader. (CMC has trained two other Yellowstone park superintendents: Edmund Rogers [1936-1957] and Bob Barbee [1982 on], who still is enthused about the fun of climbing with the Juniors.)

Mountain taxonomy specialists long have decried the proliferation of the same name. Roger Toll's 1923 book complained about it; he listed thirty-six Colorado points sharing the name "Bald," twenty-six named "Red," and twenty-two named "Sheep." The Club achieved a new name for 14,042-foot Old Baldy in 1954 — for Malcolm Lindsey, CMC climber, Denver Junior sponsor, lawyer for Denver's water board, and involved churchman. In the past two years, an unnamed peak in the Sawatch has been named for Louisa Arps and a point on Kit Carson Peak recognizes the tragedy of the *Challenger* space shot.

The Club also successfully resisted attempts to rename Mount Wilson for President Roosevelt and Mount Massive for President Kennedy. In connection with the former attempt, the Board of Directors in 1946 approved a Club policy that "use of geographic place names in Colorado be limited to those connected with Colorado history; . . . those of local significance; or honoring only those persons connected with Colorado." It also invoked the rule that a person must have been dead at least five years before such an action. Named within that five-year period, Kreutzer, Challenger, and Arps went on unnamed peaks, not on mountains already bearing long-standing, unique names.

Harriett Vaille Bouck and Edna Hendrie invited two elderly Arapaho Indians to return from their Wyoming reservation to Rocky Mountain National Park to recall the Indian history and names of the area. Oliver Toll transcribed their words and the results provided history for the Park and names for Park points. On the expedition, Shep Husted (guide), Gun Griswold, Sherman Sage, Tom Crispin (interpreter), Oliver Toll, and sitting, David Hawkins. In 1914, the ladies did not participate in the camping expedition with the Indians — only in the planning. *Photo from the National Park Service.*

Opposite Page: Climbers approach the summit of Mount Lindsey, 14,042 feet. *Photo by Spencer Swanger.*

SCHOOLS

The Colorado Mountain Club has chosen diverse methods to disseminate information. Within the Club, the schools have directly, efficaciously, improved the mountain skills of members. The schools form an essential part of the mission of the "highly individual corporation."

The first event termed a "school" occurred in 1939: a regular summer outing. The group camped at the "lovely basin at the junction of the Loch Vale and Glacier Gorge trails," said *T&T*, "flanked by two rushing streams and surrounded by tall spruce trees." (Now the Park Service would not permit camping there by forty-five people or by one.) Even though *T&T* put the word "school" in quotes, the outing did have six

Practice, Boulder Mountaineering School, May 1981. The student on the left is about to rappel while the others are prussiking up the rope. *Photo by Janet Robertson.*

days of rock and ice climbing instruction, plus climbs on which "students" put the new schooling to work.

This outing culminated with a commencement address by Dean Everett Hunt of Swarthmore College, reprinted in *T&T* (September 1939: 123). His remarks, designed "to celebrate the virtues of mountaineering as a way of life," concluded with this: "In an age of skepticism mountaineering can restore wonder and awe to living. It can restore ruggedness and independence."

Both Denver and Boulder organized formal climbing schools in 1947. By 1950, Denver offered two schools, beginning and advanced rock climbing. Beginners had to have one pair of good tennis shoes, an 80- or 120-foot $7/16$-inch nylon or manila rope, and adequate clothing. Advanced students needed a piton hammer with loop, five pitons, one to two carabiners, and a pair of strong gloves for belaying. They attended three lectures and three trips.

On a MOFA practice, class members carry a stretcher. *Photo from CMC Archives.*

The Boulder school started with twenty students: Roy Holubar, director; Werner and Rudy Schnackenberg, staff. By 1948, it took "twenty eager pupils" on five May climbing sessions. With more than its share of seductive climbing rocks, Boulder felt it should contribute as much as it could to safety on them.

Boulder's mountaineering school evolved differently from Denver's. Dan Cronin reports that the 1970 school enrolled 183 students and in 1971 Franz Mohling managed a reorganization. The Boulder school now covers the gamut of mountaineering subjects which Denver teaches in separate schools. It holds nine lectures and eight field trips in the spring, but only seven lectures and six field trips each fall. It also limits students: eighty in spring, sixty in fall. An instructors' camaraderie grows from climbing trips and feasts at St. Mary's Glacier, Vedauwoo, Wyoming, and the Brainard cabin. The Mountaineering School has been training CMC members for more than forty years. Perhaps the best indicator of the school's success is that so many students regard graduation as a beginning rather than an end. Students who enroll with an interest in mountaineering graduate with an enthusiasm for mountaineering and they act on their feelings.

Pikes Peak followed the lead of the northerly CMC groups and began to sponsor a rock climbing school, one which attracts members from the El Pueblo Group as well. In the sixties they had an advantage — instructors included the professional climbers at Fort Carson.

By 1977, that first Denver school had the title, "Basic Mountaineering," and discussed things like boots and boot buying, map reading, lightning, and leadership. It included eight field trips for rock climbing, rappelling, snow and ice, and a high peak climb. Students even had to pass a final exam!

The Denver Group decided to teach its members more about avalanches after members started an avalanche on a 1976 Club trip. With the help of the ski patrol, Club leaders Mike Foster, Piet Hondius, and John McCorkle initiated an avalanche awareness course. They redesigned a ski patrol course from an emphasis on downhill skiing to one designed for backcountry skiers, and now it teaches 300 people per year about the hazards of the back country in winter. *T&T* carries a steady drumbeat of articles on avalanches and winter safety, so that members at the least have access to information on safe winter mountaineering.

Several Club groups offer first aid courses and encourage members to acquire that important backcountry skill. Denver calls it "Mountain

Boulder Group rescue practice: Tom Hornbein carries an unidentified climber down the face of a cliff (1952). *Photo by Phil Robertson.*

Oriented First Aid," (MOFA) and drew ideas for the format from former Club president Clint Kelley — who left Denver for the Seattle Mountaineers in the early 1970s. The program has three parts: Red Cross standard first aid, CPR certification, and mountain emergencies. The third emphasizes problem solving, prevention, improvisation, assessment, and TLC (Tender Loving Care). A graduation hike with the Alpine Rescue Group concludes the course. The school even sponsors regular B classification MOFA hikes open to any Club member.

Nelson Chenkin took a CPR course through the Fort Collins Group. On a talus slope in the Rawah Wilderness in 1979, he, wife Jude, and a friend encountered a thunderstorm. Lightning struck Jude; "her feet lay in a hole 18 inches deep where football-sized rocks had been blasted from the earth. I tried my CPR, moving desperately from chest compression to resuscitation. After just a few attempts I heard Jude gasp for air . . . we sat in the falling rain watching her ashy complexion begin to return to normal." After a helicopter pickup and five days in the hospital, she recovered. CMC has good reasons for urging members to know first aid.

Most Club schools teach about how to do things in the mountains; few have taught about the mountains themselves. Russ Allen's 1987

Instruction in tying climbing knots in climbing ropes. People (from the early 1950s) are unidentified except the second from the right (Rusty Bailey). *Photo from CMC Archives.*

Students await their turn at the belay tower used in the Boulder Mountaineering School. *Photo by Janet Robertson.*

The Denver Group's Technical
Ice Climbing School practices
in Ten Mile Canyon:
Steve Kaye.
Photo by Paul Svetlik.

Alpine Glacial Geology course did the latter: Russ taught about the alpine landscape and how glaciations, past and present, influenced that landscape. Of course, the Club has for years scheduled nature observing trips with experts on flowers, birds, and geology — informal schools.

Lorena Darby said in *T&T*, "Leadership includes not only the responsibility for 'showing the way' but trying to assure that those led enjoy the outing. It helps if the leader knows a bit of the history . . . geology . . . flowers . . . a few of the animals besides chipmunks, and a few of the birds other than robins . . . the Longs Peak Group is attempting to encourage an 'I can' attitude among its members. 'I can' learn . . . history . . . 'I can' see on-the-spot places I've seen from a distance for a long time; 'I can' sharpen my awareness of the need to conserve and protect areas I've hiked through . . . 'I can' enjoy the feeling of companionship that goes with the sharing of a hiking experience; 'I can' go farther the next time. . . ."

Blanca Peak (left), 14,345 feet, showing its imposing north face. *Photo by Harry Standley.*

Chapter Three

"To stimulate the public interest in our mountain area . . ."

To inform the public about our mountains, the Club, of course, has issued the series of publications described above. It also sponsors the incredible series of trips, winter and summer, which entice so many members of the public into membership.

Club groups have for years sponsored public lectures, slide shows, and movie programs about the mountains. The Denver Group now provides them semimonthly, the other groups on a less regular basis. Lectures cover climbing, trekking, travel, wildlife, and just plain good photography.

The Club had a long personal relationship with William Henry Jackson, famous photographer of Mount of the Holy Cross and other early mountain scenes of the West. Jackson went on several CMC outings in the 1920s, and the Club made him an honorary member in 1938. Half a year before that happy event, Jackson had written to the Club about an item in *T&T* which "states that 'second hand sleeping bags are greatly in demand.' The last time I used my bed roll, tarp, sleeping bag, blankets &c. was at the [CMC] Ice Lakes Camp of 1932. Since then it has been an incumberance and of no possible use. So I am sending it to the Club, express pre-paid, to be disposed of as you think best — preferably to some boy or girl whose love of the out-of-doors in the various activities of the Club is greater than the means for satisfying it. . . ." The Club gave it to CMC Junior member Lloyd Glasier, who first used it on a "grand outing" to Snowmass. Club secretary Evelyn Runnette optimistically commented to Jackson, "I know that he enjoyed it and appreciated your gift. I hope he wrote you!"

The Jackson association stemmed from a widespread Club appreciation of photographic efforts. Early members exchanged snapshots and ordered copies from each other — one reason the Club's early days are so well-memorialized pictorially. Pikes Peaker Harry Standley photographed the Fourteeners, and members' scrapbooks bulged with those still superb pictures. (For a while the Pikes Peak Group library resided in his photographic shop.) Trail & Timberline offers a forum for photographers' products. The covers and often the inside present a striking collection of mountain photography. Most pictures appear in black-and-white, though since 1970 two or three T&Ts have used color photographs from CMC exhibits.

The Club has conducted annual photographic exhibits since 1918 and color slide shows since 1940. Presenting the best of mountain photography, the mounted prints travel the state, on exhibit in various Club cities. KRMA-TV aired the Club's fortieth slide show in 1977, a grand way to tell about the mountains.

In 1953, 260 attended the Annual Kodachrome Show in Denver, and

Climbing party on the Knife Edge, Capitol Peak, 14,130 feet, circa 1929.
Photo courtesy of Polly Bouck.

Trip number 40 ascended Grays and Torreys peaks, 14,270 feet and 14,267 feet, respectively, on July 26, 1914. *Photo by Dr. Edward Jackson, from CMC Archives.*

more saw it in Fort Collins and Colorado Springs. (In 1954, the Club recognized commercial competition by renaming it the Annual Color Slide Show.)

As one of its first projects, the Club installed a mountain name indicator in Denver's Cheesman Park. Removed in 1980, the remnants remain in the Club archives, waiting for someone to resurrect it, perhaps as a coffee table. The Longs Peak Group also built one in 1980, when it presented a plaque to the James Hamm Nature Park which portrayed the Longmont mountain skyline. It showed the names, location, and elevation of all the peaks in the outline. "Plaque" seems a modest title for it — a structure made of a redwood slab eight feet long, two and a half feet wide, and two inches thick, with a plexiglass cover for the peak identifications.

The Club has had a mountaineering library since the beginning, and it contains a wealth of books — 1,500 of them — of interest to mountain-goers. The Club library resides in the clubrooms, where members may browse through books and periodicals or check them out (in person or by mail). Libraries don't just happen; Helen Stiles-Wainwright managed it for over twenty years, as it matured. Her expertise was even

Lenore Greene signs register on Grays Peak, May 30, 1962. *Photo by Gwen Toepfer.*

Original register with metal canister. *Photo from CMC Archives.*

recognized by a national library association. The Boulder Group has a similar, but smaller collection of books in its Club office. Pikes Peak, too, has one, which it disbanded during its hard times and then reconstituted.

The Denver library holds more than books; it has scrapbooks of early Club history, various mementos, and a unique resource about Colorado mountains: high peak registers.

Perhaps the folks who sign them don't need their interest stimulated, but the Club has installed climbers' registers on summits since the first days. The original canisters for the registers, hefty steel tubes, attracted lightning bolts, supposedly. They also did not always stay closed, and some registers furnished non-nutritious sustenance for rodents which ventured to 14,000 feet. Some Club scientist should study the identity and food requirements of those hungry varmints.

The present registers, of plastic, solve those problems, but do not solve the problem of two-footed varmints who squirrel the registers into their packs to take as souvenirs. One wonders about the ultimate disposition of registers which depart that way. The proper route for the registers is to the clubrooms — where Club climbers deliver filled-up registers for filing and future reference (read on to see how the Conservation Committee used them).

Sometimes the registers return home in shreds (or sometimes the souvenir seekers take only the cover page). Club secretary Sally Richards, in the June 1981 *T&T*, listed twenty-seven Club climbers and asked them if they remembered what peak they climbed on the dates listed. She hoped, with their help, to link peak to register pages (some of which she described as "cony-chewed, vandalized, ribaldized pieces of crud").

Jerry Cajori enjoys a view of Courthouse Mountain, 12,152 feet, and Chimney Peak, 11,781 feet, on the 1965 Cimarron outing. *Photo by Elwyn Arps.*

Chapter Four

"To encourage the preservation of forests, flowers and natural scenery . . ."

Our 1912 founders did not use the words "conservation" and "environment" and "ecology" — those words had not yet come into common usage. But they expressed the aims of today's environmental movement simply and directly. They and their successors have, for the most part, carried out the founders' directive effectively.

Environmental issues come both big and small. Some are remembered, some are forgotten. It would take a month of research to gather the details of that long-forgotten 1921 bill which threatened the national parks ("iniquitous" according to a call to action in *T&T*), successfully opposed by the Club. Yet we all can bask in the pride of belonging to a Club which led the effort to establish Rocky Mountain National Park. The Club participated in "drawing of the bill for the Rocky Mountain National Park and participation in the campaign for its adoption." Having as its legislative chairman Morrison Shafroth, the lawyer son of a U.S. senator from Colorado, no doubt helped the Club's efforts. In that one task, the "highly individual corporation" left a lasting and memorable legacy to our state and country.

Other early campaigns seem, today, somewhat quixotic.

The Fort Collins Group in the 1920s fenced an old cottonwood tree with barbed wire and erected a sign around it. Why? Laura Makepeace reported that it "had been a Cheyenne Indian council tree in the days of Chief Friday. In the 1920s, old-timers still remembered him and his tribe wandering through this part of the state. Cattle were pasturing in the field where the tree stood and it was slowly being damaged," hence the fencing. However, "Nearly 20 years later a passing C&S train sent sparks into the branches and the tree was entirely destroyed."

In furtherance of the preservation of the natural scenery, the Club

In furtherance of the preservation of the natural scenery, the Club went directly to the users in order to protect the high country. The Club prepared "Good Woodsman" signs and other signs admonishing mountain users to leave a clean camp. They posted these signs throughout the Colorado Rockies; some remain today, as in Genesee Mountain Park.

"Wildflower Excursion," a 115-mile scenic trip advertised by the Colorado Midland Railway for $1.00 (50 cents for children between five and twelve years).

went directly to the users in order to protect the high country. The Club prepared "Good Woodsman" signs and other signs admonishing mountain users to leave a clean camp. They posted these signs throughout the Colorado Rockies; some remain today, as in Genesee Mountain Park. Today the Forest Service pleads with the users not to start forest fires, but seventy years ago, the CMC sought to persuade the users to honor the mountains in other ways as well.

The Club put out other signs: in 1920 the Forest Service invoiced the Club for $155.60 to cover 155 signs (65 "Spare the Flowers," 65 "Protect the Birds," and 25 campsite signs).

A major campaign involved the Colorado columbine. Some tourist companies advertised trips on which their customers could pick bouquets of flowers, and illustrated the ads with lovely damsels whose faces barely showed behind the load of columbines they held. The Club persuaded the legislature to enact a statute which prohibited picking any more than *twenty-five* columbines in one day. Letters went out: "It has been called to our attention that an automobile licensed in your name has been seen in the mountains carrying quantities of wild-flowers. We write to ask your cooperation in protecting the wild-flowers." And an answer from one recipient denying his car had been even as far as the Motor Club, "and we never even picked a dandelion, your argument is good however."

The Club sent eighty-two letters in 1924 (including one to the com-

Columbine Law

"*Section 1.* It is hereby declared to be the duty of all citizens of this State to protect the white and lavender Columbine, *Aquilegia caerulea*, (the State Flower) from needless destruction or waste.

"*Section 2.* It shall be unlawful for any person to tear the said flowers up by the roots when grown or growing upon any State, school, or other public lands, or in any public highway or other public place, or to pick or gather upon any such public lands or in any such public highway or place more than twenty-five stems, buds or blossoms of such flower in any one day, and it shall also be unlawful for any person to pick or gather such flower upon private lands without the consent of the owner thereof first had or obtained.

"*Section 3.* Any person who shall violate any provision of Section 2 of this Act shall be deemed guilty of a misdemeanor and upon conviction shall be fined not less than five dollars nor more than fifty dollars."

Strongly Supported by
ALL LOYAL COLORADOANS

The text of the columbine law.

mittee chairman's cousin) but only fourteen in 1925 after passage of the columbine bill.

This seems staggering to us today, but it must have worked. Now we think the columbine flourishes throughout our mountain country — but apparently not as once it did, covering acres and acres. Bill Ramaley said in *T&T* that we can't imagine "how the mountain meadows of Colorado once were blue with columbines, how flaming red wood lilies lighted up the shadowy places, and how delicate orchids bloomed everywhere. Only a few places, such as isolated parts of Rocky Mountain National Park, are left to suggest the past glory of our native wildflowers."

The Club also exercised a huge effort to eradicate billboards from the Denver Mountain Parks and elsewhere. Club files bulge with letters to companies which advertised on billboards, and of the advertisers' acquiescence to the firm though courteous importunities of Harry Field for the Club.

Field, in the real estate business, addressed a letter on May 22, 1922, presumably to the businesses involved, about the vision which created the mountain parks, and stated that the next issue of *T&T* would call to the attention of its 1,200 members the names of "five business concerns who have not yet removed their advertising signs from the Entrance to our Mountain Parks." On June 12, 1922, he wrote to Thomas Cusack Company on behalf of the Club "to extend you our very hearty thanks for your splendid co-operation in the removal of the signs at the Gateway to the Mountain Parks, at the foot of Lookout Mountain . . . in time for the Annual Field Day of the Mountain Club. We had about four hundred members present (!) and recognition of your courtesy and co-operation was given by the President, and responded to by hearty approval of the members there gathered."

The Pikes Peak Group lobbied El Paso County commissioners to ban billboards from county highways and boycotted businesses that ignored the ruling.

The Denver committee's file stops in 1925, but in 1937, state senator Rudolph Johnson — of the Boulder CMC — introduced a billboard bill; it apparently died. The fight resumed after World War II, but with less success.

The Fort Collins Group persuaded its city council to declare the city a bird sanctuary — an effort reinforced in 1987 when Fort Collins became the first city in the country designated by the National Institute for Urban Wildlife as an "Urban Wildlife Sanctuary."

Some of the group gathered at the site of the first tree planting in 1946. *Photo from CMC Archives.*

In 1936, the directors listened to statements for and against the transmountain diversions of the Colorado-Big Thompson project. Ward Bannister, prominent Denver water lawyer, and Edmund Rogers, then superintendent of Rocky Mountain National Park, respectively presented the pros and cons. After due consideration the directors adopted a statement endorsing the inviolability of national parks and opposing the tunnels and diversions of the Big Thompson project.

T&T reported little about this branch of Club activities for a decade and many members forgot, or never knew of, the Club's early commitment to nature protection. Fort Collins resolved in 1951 that the piñon pine grove northwest of the city receive recognition as a state park. This finally occurred — thirty years later.

Club members put in a huge effort on the annual tree planting weekend. It began in 1946 with 150 members working on South Boulder Creek near Rollinsville. In 1950, 160 planters from five of the seven groups (absent, Colorado College Juniors and Huerfano) came. In 1951, the gang planted 11,000 lodgepole pines. For refreshments, Alex Carson manned the fire for hot coffee and Cedric Kaub, expert packer, lashed, the same way he packed horses, "large metal water and punch containers

Club members plant trees at the Mammoth Burn near Apex. *Photo from CMC Archives.*

in the back seat of his convertible." For sixteen years Club members planted trees in a series of Forest Service-selected sites west of Boulder, the last one near Gold Hill. A short-lived tree planting echo in 1968-1969 found Club members planting skunkbush along Denver-area freeways.

The Club's nature protection reached its low point in 1954 when controversy erupted over a dam proposed at Echo Park in Dinosaur National Monument. The Club had had a part in the establishment of this national monument in 1935-1937. Edmund Rogers described the Yampa Canyon area in a long article for *T&T* readers. The Club conducted a reconnaissance trip September 5-12, 1936.

When the proposal to dam the confluence of the Green and Yampa surfaced in 1954, the Club lacked a concensus. The issue generated spirited discussions within the Club. *T&T* carried articles for and against the dam, and the Board of Directors polled the membership by post card as to whether or not CMC should take a stand against the dam. Of the 761 cards mailed out, 334 were returned. The vote opposed the dam 224 to 89 (21 votes on neither side). *T&T* reported: "After considerable discussion, including a comment that a 44 percent return is better than usual, the Board of Directors voted that, since only 30 percent of the membership expressed opposition to the dam, the Colorado Mountain Club should not take a stand either for or against construction of Echo Park dam." Another factor in the decision: the directors feared a public stand might jeopardize its tax-exempt status. (The IRS never actually granted this status; the Club applied for it but the IRS refused because it viewed an organization which conducted square dances as a social club.)

Where the government proposed a dam: Steamboat Rock, at the confluence of the Yampa and Green rivers in Dinosaur National Monument. *Photo by H.L. Standley.*

Fortunately for that unique piece of Colorado river scenery, other organizations, in-state and out, succeeded in thwarting the dam. The Pikes Peak and Boulder groups maintained their opposition separately and communicated the same to the dam builders. A postscript: In 1956, the board declined to take action on a proposal to convert Dinosaur from a national monument to a national park. They left it up to local groups to endorse such an action.

From that point the Club's conservation/environmental activity, as begun by and envisioned by its founders, has soared. Although *T&T* carried no conservation news (except about tree planting) from 1953 to 1956, the seeds for reconstituting the Club's preservation concern had been planted.

Roger Fuehrer and Dick Guadagno revived the Conservation Committee in 1961; this committee first addressed that old CMC nemesis: billboards. It helped pass a state law which had some impact on improving the natural view from the state's highways and byways. It advocated painting microwave and power line towers to blend in with the surroundings.

CMC had a major part in the enactment of the Wilderness Act of 1964. Chairman Aspinall of the congressional committee which controlled this legislation came from Colorado. At a Denver hearing, many CMC members testified for the bill — including a panel of five Juniors. Having strong wilderness advocates from his state startled him and helped immeasurably to achieve that milestone achievement.

In a turn-around from the Echo Park controversy, the Club acted vigorously to oppose the insensitive proposal to put dams into the Grand Canyon. It also helped to persuade the federal and state governments not to route I-70 up steep, avalanche-prone South Willow Creek through the Eagles Nest Wilderness. As a result, Red Buffalo Pass remains part of a spectacular wilderness and Vail Pass hosts an award-winning interstate highway, safe from Colorado's testy avalanche hazards.

During the 1960s, Club groups began litter trips — to pick up, not to drop, the stuff that less sensitive mountain-goers left along the trails. Dick Lamm and Dottie Vennard (Lamm) authored a *T&T* article which

Dick Lamm hiked (here, to Bluebird Lake in 1965) and climbed with the Club, including several high peaks on the Peruvian outing. He wrote many *T&T* articles on conservation subjects and subsequently became state legislator and Colorado governor. *Photo by Sam Alfend.*

advocated that Club members pack out what they pack in, from bottles and cans to cigarette butt filters. In 1968, the Pikes Peak Group removed thirty bushels of litter from the Barr Trail. The Enos Mills Group sponsored a trip on June 12, 1982, which garnered eighty pickers from six groups; this first Club cleanup in a national park went to twenty-six different areas in Rocky Mountain National Park.

After the inspiring fiftieth anniversary conference at Estes Park, the Club sponsored a series of open space conferences. Concrete results followed: the Colorado Open Space Council (COSC) organized and began coordinating the groups in the state with a commitment to environmental integrity. Prominent state and national speakers prodded attendees to more effective efforts and to more issues.

COSC was not the first statewide conservation umbrella group. The Colorado State Conservation Council had an apparently short life beginning in 1936. Affiliate groups included the CMC, the Colorado Bird Club, the Colorado Federation of Garden Clubs, the Chamber of Commerce, the Junior Chamber, and the Craig Lions Club. Perhaps that diversity of groups had a diversity of viewpoints which prevented any effective conservation accomplishments; in any event, *T&T* referred to it only twice.

Conservation Chairman Estella Leopold and Club President-elect Al Auten presented to Rick Bradley (center) the CMC Conservation Award at the 1966 Open Space Conference. The Club commended "his extraordinarily effective work at publicizing nationally the threat to the Grand Canyon posed by the Central Arizona Project dams." *Photo by Hugh E. Kingery.*

Then in 1972, a Club-members-only open space conference directed that Club conservation concentrate on issues which directly affect Club interests: advocacy of wilderness, use and care of the back country, and the effects of such land uses as mining operations and water planning upon our mountain recreation and backcountry areas.

A membership poll in 1985 supported that viewpoint: 85 percent of those responding (270 members, 3 percent of the Club) supported either the present or more Club involvement in environmental issues. They favored action in forest planning, wilderness, land access, but suggested going easy on water rights, mining, and air quality.

The first result of attention to Club concerns was an *Outdoor Code* — 73,500 copies published in 1972. It has not continued as a Club publication, however.

Conservation has commanded much attention from the State Board in the last two decades. A 1977 Board resolution declared that recreational activities constitute a major Colorado industry. The Club issued a report in 1984 on the economics of recreation (meaning high peaks, scenic areas, clean air, wildlife, etc.). The report identified a four-billion-dollar business related to outdoor recreation. It calculated the economic benefits of climbing — using the number of ascents and home residences of climbers of certain peaks — derived from peak registers deposited in the clubrooms. It called upon the state government to calculate more accurately the contribution of recreational activities to the state's economy.

In 1978, *T&T* talked about the negative impacts of Two Forks dam, in connection with an unsuccessful opposition to the Foothills Water Plant. *T&T* contains the same message in 1987.

The Club made a major commitment in 1981 by hiring a paid, part-time conservation staff director, Anne Vickery of Boulder. Beginning at $500 per month, she has represented the Club on the forefront of *mountain* environmental issues like wilderness, national forests, air quality, access to public lands, etc.

* * *

The Club has achieved some notable successes — Rocky Mountain National Park and the Wilderness Act, for example. The Conservation Committee reported an important one in 1986: our region of the Forest Service no longer offers timber sales if the cost of the road exceeds the potential return from the timber sale. Some activities exhibit less success: because of the negative impact on the Holy Cross Wilderness, the Club in 1986 joined a lawsuit in Colorado Water Court against Aurora and Colorado Springs, which propose a giant water diversion project called Homestake II.

But will success spoil the land? The Club reported in 1986, "Wilderness, seen as a haven for hikers, backpackers, campers, hunters, outfitters, now shows severe impact from recreational use such as soil compaction and erosion, and elimination of vegetation." (No more outings at Snowmass Lake or the Needles, or other wilderness sites.) The CMC has started "to work with the Forest Service to try to reduce recreational impacts, reverse man-made erosional processes, and to bring back natural vegetation. It appears that while the federal agencies have started a shift away from public use toward preservation, this trend does not embrace wilderness water." The enormous pressures from the burgeoning water developing interests led to a CMC statement which declared that headwater wilderness is protected by the Wilderness Act, and only by presidential proclamation can water development proceed in a wilderness.

The Mountain Club at Fern Lake Lodge. *Photo from CMC Archives.*

The Club *should* have an interest in these issues. *T&T* reported in 1978 that over 70 percent of Club trips go into Forest Service roadless areas, and that a Forest Service proposal that year protected only 17 percent of them.

A CMC survey proved that climbers and hikers, in-state and out, make a significant contribution to the Colorado economy. Siesta on the summit of Sugarloaf, October 13, 1962. *Photo by Gwen Toepfer.*

Chapter Five

". . . to render accessible alpine attractions of the region."

An annual schedule of 2,271 trips attests to the smashing success of the Club in this field. It took sixteen years to run the first 500 trips: now that many occur in the space of two months. Different reporters choose different ways to describe that success.

Mary Shirer reported on a 1950 Pikes Peak trip, "The day was so perfect that the nine participants could not determine the time of year, although the calendar told us it was February 8. Pearl Turner had the honor of luring the first woodtick of the season."

In 1955, *T&T* reporter Carolyn Campbell said, "Longer registers and thinner boot soles indicate a successful season for CMC members, and the proof is in the trip reports." Stan Stortz claimed that in 1969, "350 Denver Group backpackers hauled 3¼ tons of equipment about 140 miles of trail to gain 23,000 feet of elevation so they could sleep in the snow and rain." At one annual dinner a Denver Group chairman said that his members had climbed the equivalent of six and one-half Mount Everests.

The Pikes Peak *T&T* writer in 1954 reported that the Group climbed four peaks and "we have studied geology, plant life, and electric power generation. We have stretched our muscles on rock climbs and relaxed toasting marshmallows before an open fire. We have, in short, enjoyed ourselves, our companions, and our surroundings."

In 1984, the Club summer schedule involved 9,630 user days in national forests. That amount of usage shows the importance to Club members of the Conservation Committee efforts to monitor forest management.

Opposite Page: Climbing party on Longs Peak, 1930s. *Photo by Glenn Gebhardt.*

These trips sponsored by the Club serve their purposes well. Witness the comment in an article on the Glacier National Park outing by Ethel Francisco in 1958: "I am one of the many who have been greatly benefited by the club. I have written this in appreciation for all the kindness I have received from the club members and for all the friends I have made in it. I hope I have proved that the CMC continues to fulfill its aim to make the far-distant mountain areas accessible to those who, without the club, could never enjoy them."

Janet Chatin, in describing her first climb with the Club in 1927, of West Spanish Peak, said that after the climb, she was a "different person." Not knowing anything about "high climbing," she remembers learning from Carl Blaurock about huckleberry, serviceberry, Oregon grape, and kinnikinnick. "I asked (being young and wanting to make the grade as an interested, prospective member) if one could use them for jelly. He wasn't sure but he thought that if the Indians could use kinnikinnick for smoking, these berries could put a kick in the jelly." They made the top, and she vividly remembered the downward trek: "stiff legs in knee-length boots with heavy soles, dangled rather than stepped."

In 1941, Club members referred to overnights, like this one to Jackson Creek on May 25, as "Carry-all trips." *Photo from CMC Archives.*

Today the thousands of trips cater to eager beavers and to huffers and puffers, and as Stan Boucher and Bill Arnold said, the trips run smoothly, Club members enjoy them, and it is difficult to write about them.

OUTINGS

"The leadership of the club has come directly from those who have attended the statewide outings. I believe the club outings have an energizing effect upon the club." Thus C. Earl Davis, 1939 Club pres-

Now we call them "Backpacks" and have equipment designed to make the burden less exhausting. Fording Texas Creek, Sawatch Range, 1975. *Photo by Janet Robertson.*

Climbing Aztec on the 1920 San Juan outing.
Photo from CMC Archives.

"Batter up" — 1920 CMC San Juan outing. *Photo from CMC Archives.*

The umpire, Billy Myatt, 1920 CMC San Juan outing.
Photo from CMC Archives.

ident, explained why outings have formed such an important part of the Club's activities.

In the early days, the business of the Club was to get Club members into the back country. From the first year the Club sponsored one- or two-week outings which did that business well. But, as Earl Davis observed, the outings also did business for the highly individual corporation.

These outings highlighted the summer season, and still do. They offer good climbing with good leaders, good hiking with equally good leaders, and even some flower ambles. A unique spirit pervades the camp; outing-goers remember their experiences with special fondness and pride.

The first outing went to Bear Creek Basin on Mount Evans. The 1914 outing to the Never Summer Range, now in Rocky Mountain National Park, had a traveling camp, and on that one, allegedly, the cook took after a cook's helper with a carving knife. Billy Myatt also reminisced about a memorable bit of cooking on that one. The group gathered pails of huckleberries, which they presented to the cook for cobbler. Waiting with anticipation, they piled their plates high with luscious-looking cobbler. "We cut into the heavenly crust, exposing the rich fruit dripping with royal purple juice. We lifted the first bite to our lips — and our expressions changed suddenly from eager anticipation, through disbelief, to the stark realization that something was terribly wrong. This was not the rich flavor we had anticipated — instead our mouths were full of the taste of coal oil and axle grease." It turned out the cook had greased the pans with kerosene.

The most famous of the early outings transported eighty-four folks into Chicago Basin in 1920. It also transported a stove. Billy Myatt explained: Schroeder, the cook, was a typically temperamental chef, "particular to a fault, a skilled skillet slinger and master meat man, to whom every detail was a principle. He insisted on having a better stove than the one he'd been using, so we gave $20.00 and carte blanche to select one. There we erred. Not the carte blanche but the $20.00, because he found an enormous secondhand kitchen range complete with stovepipe and water reservoir at the side, and it must have weighed at least 350 pounds, sans lids, sans grids, sans doors, sans everything loose — and that was to go into the great San Juan; and it did . . . two mules carried it, tandem, the stove swung between them.

"But what meals Schroeder coaxed out of it! And what satisfaction he got out of it. A true artist.

"Came the end of the outing; time to pack out; at the suggestion [of the packer] we left it [there] intact — grids, lids, doors, and reservoir. We had had our money's worth out of it.

"1927 and back to Chicago Basin. You guessed it! The stove was still there — grids, lids, doors, and reservoir — complete. Schroeder was with us again and his delight on finding it was unbounded, for by digging out the accumulated sand and other debris it was serviceable

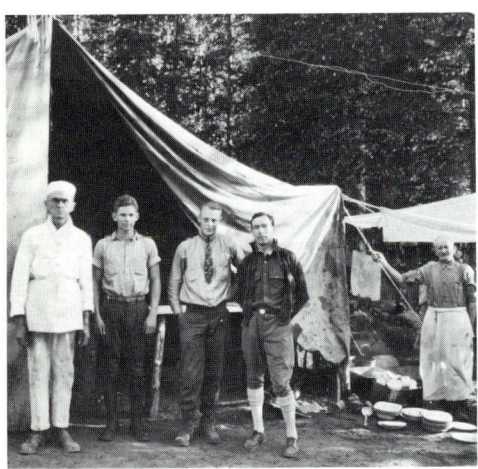

As secretaries vest the clubrooms with personality, so cooks have anchored the outings: Schroeder, Ted Lee (imported from Canada with certificates to the Immigration Office of his unique ability to fill a job no U.S. citizen could), and now, Mibby Lewis. *Above:* Schroeder and cook crew. *Photo by Harry Standley. Below:* Ted Lee serves coffee to Anne Frantz on a 1955 Lake O'Hara outing. *Photo by Louise Roloff.*

for another season."

Spence Swanger mused about the 1934 Blue Lakes (Sneffels area) outing: "Imagine the thrill of being able to establish a base camp in Colorado's Rockies from where a dozen first ascents could be had."

1953 Needles outing leader Henry Buchtel said that "local ground rules permit use of columbines as handholds, at least on Pigeon Peak." (It's lucky that the columbine committee didn't get his license plate number.)

Dining tent, early outing. Also entitled "The End." *Photo from CMC Archives.*

Sunday dinner on the outing. On left side, Malcolm Collier, Billy Myatt, Mary Spreng, Fred Spreng *et al.*; on right side from front, Howard Vaile, 5th and 6th, Karl Arndt, Mary Cronin, *et al. Photo from CMC Archives.*

The statistics show that the San Juan Mountains have attracted the most outings, twenty-two, with the Needles, Sneffels, and Lake City areas drawing the most. Other statistics: seven outings to the Front Range, the last to Argentine Pass in 1944; six to the Wind River Range, and four to the Tetons of Wyoming; five to Ice Mountain in the Sawatch, all since 1957.

Legendary Snowmass Lake has hosted the most official outings — but none since 1957. CMC and the Forest Service noted the impact of CMC's scores of campers (to say nothing of others who arrive on their own) on the fragile wilderness; no one now can camp within one-quarter mile of the lake. CMC recognizes the inappropriateness of conducting dozens of people at a time into wilderness. Now the Forest Service won't permit parties larger than ten into the wilderness.

CMC has now expanded its horizons to the rest of the world. The first out-of-state outing, in 1926, went to Glacier National Park. The first year of two outings, 1954, saw trips to Holy Cross and Mount Rainier. The first out-of-country outing went to the Canadian Rockies (Lake O'Hara) in 1955. They used nearly all their supplies: the only thing left at the end was a half case of ketchup and a full case of sardines. Now foreign outings come almost annually and have gone to Peru, New Zealand, Japan, Iceland, Africa, and all over Europe.

In 1987, the summer schedule announced a dozen outings and three expeditions. They went to Scotland, Peru, Yugoslavia and Italy, Madeira, and Ecuador, as well as to more mundane places like Alaska, the Green River, the Big Horn Mountains in Wyoming, and the Grand Canyon. An "in-state" outing camped near the Eagles Nest Wilderness.

Originally the leaders volunteered their time, but now most receive a stipend (not much considering the work involved) or a free trip. Originally, too, outings took people to places they could not attain on their own, furnished experienced, capable leaders, and especially provided someone else to cook the meals.

Backpacking equipment was primitive, transportation slow, and logistics difficult. The Club performed a service not available as readily then as now. Today the Forest Service has put limits on the numbers of people who can pack into the back country. The Club runs its outings (and even its day trips) as an outfitter with a permit from the Forest Service. By coordinating with the Forest Service and by limiting numbers, Club trips leave less impact on the mountains.

Outings offer the kind of mountain experience which differs in quality from more commercially oriented trips. Recent outings have varied the early pattern. Some require participants to bring and cook their own food, others their own transportation (canoe trips to Minnesota), and still others both transportation and fuel (ski trips to Yellowstone). All of them, though, still involve dedicated leaders and incomparable companionship.

That, of course, is what the CMC is all about.

The Club has also sponsored, in part, several high climbing expeditions. The 1951 climb of Mount McKinley was really sponsored by Denver University and the Boston Museum of Science, but five of the eight scientific and exploring climbers came from CMC. One, Barry Bishop, went on to ascend Mount Everest, with two other CMCers, Dick Pownall and Al Auten (subsequently Club president).

The Club has sponsored expeditions such as the 1982 attempt on

English outing, valley near Wasdale, July 9, 1972. Al Mullen, Jane Schnackenberg, Elinor Kingery. *Photo by Elwyn Arps.*

Dick Lamm crossing a crevasse near the summit of 19,785-foot Mount Tocllaraju, Cordillera Blanca Range, Peru, 1963. *Photo by Sue O'Brien.*

Dale Johnson at the Tocllaraju high camp, 17,500 feet, Peru, 1963. *Photo by Sue O'Brien.*

Kongur, 25,325 feet high in Xinjiang Province, China; trekkers accompanied the expedition. Glenn Porzak (former Boulder Conservation chair and CMC president) has in the past decade carried the CMC climbing banner to major summits all over the world.

WINTER OUTINGS

In 1916, the Club expanded its outing horizons to wintertime and started to sponsor winter outings at Fern Lake Lodge, in newly established Rocky Mountain National Park. An anonymous Club historian, trying to drum up customers for the 1921 outing, explained: "The much be-garmented crowd, laden with snowshoes, skis, smoked glasses and the small necessities of living, make the trip from Denver to Estes Park by automobile. From Estes Park stages carry them to the Brinwood Hotel, where the snowshoeing begins. Mush — mush — mush — mush — up the frozen waterway, one eye attentive to the scientific placing of the snowshoes, the other to the beauties of the snow-decked

CMC conducted an outing to Peru in 1963 led by Harold Walton. Members tallied eighty-one summit climbs to peaks over 17,000 feet. One campsite lay in a high valley below Chinchey, one of the ten peaks. *Photo by Dave and Freddy Carter.*

Bob Fernie and Bob Clifton looked like aviators on March 9, 1930, when they climbed over the divide from Tolland to West Portal. *Photo from Boulder CMC Archives.*

landscape. If fortune and the weather be favorable, late afternoon shows them Fern Lodge and a cheery welcome within its hospitable walls. . . . . For two days high carnival reigns on the lakes. . . . The spectacular skiing is found higher up in the country above Odessa. Here several courses, the longest perhaps a half mile with a drop of four hundred feet, terminate in a sweeping basin. It is here that the novices, while gathering valuable experience for themselves, provide the others with much merriment."

At first they traveled by snowshoe and dragged their skis behind them by ropes put through holes in the tips. The outing committee in 1922 announced that "anyone desiring to travel on skis alone, should hobble them with a rope or a carpet sack . . . and he will find no difficulty."

"Soon," reported Louisa Arps and Elinor Kingery in *High Country Names,* "many walked up the trail on skis, with ropes or canvas bags fastened to the skis to prevent slipping."

Exuberant skiers spread over the landscape, practicing on the "baby, adolescent, mature or very mature courses" — telemarking, jumping, romping in the snow, or simply marveling on snowshoe trips through the woods. Sally Vaille (Mrs. Edmund Rogers), reporting on the 1922 outing, claimed, "There was a continual embarrassment of riches, one

having to choose between bumping the bumps on the toboggan, skiing, following the winding trails to Odessa or Spruce Lakes, or exploring Spruce Canon.

"The loveliest of all trips," she said, "is Odessa by moonlight when all the marvels of the winter world are covered with a soft radiance and one either weaves up the creek-bed with its weird, fantastic, fluffy rocks or swings up over the ski trail." They never forgot those moonlit ski ventures, whether they skied well or not.

After eighteen years, poor snow conditions forced cancellation of one outing and discouraged people from registering for the next; 1934's rescheduled outing was the last. Movies, taken by Hugh M. Kingery, hilariously record some of the antics from this era; copies reside at the State Historical Society and (soon) at Vail's Ski Hall of Fame.

The Park Service in 1976 finally razed Fern Lake Lodge as inappropriate in a national park wilderness. After World War II, huts began to spring up in other ski places. The Juniors held outings at a water board cabin on Jones Pass — they could drive to that one. Aspen area huts, holding from four to twenty, beckon Club skiers on weekend and week-long trips.

In recent winters, organized winter outings have explored the winter wonders of Yellowstone National Park. CMCers explore the geyser basins and thermal pools by ski and by snowshoe.

CABINS

Club winter activities have had, as one center of focus, various cabins. The Fern Lake Lodge and Fort Collins' leased lodge at Chambers Lake were the first.

Irene Reese recounted the Chambers Lake ritual. CMCers moved into the cabin around Armistice Day. They piled "stuff" on a big sled, if enough snow covered the ground. Stuff included firewood, hams and a slab of bacon, boxes of bread, and canned goods. Eggs in waterglass, butter in brine. When winter came they usually could drive within

Opposite Page: Notchtop dominates the trail from Fern Lake to Odessa Lake. Photo by H. M. Kingery.

four miles. The trips and warm friendship engendered by this association enriched the lives of all who participated. But after twenty-five years, in 1956, the group let the lease expire because most skiers preferred the "ballroom ski areas."

The Club has used a succession of other cabins as well. Longevity goes to Boulder's Brainard Lake cabin. Jan Robertson's *Front Rangers* explains that Professor Van Valkenburg ("Van") of the Chemistry Department at the University proposed it in 1927. Van, Gayle Waldrop, and Charles Hutchison planned and organized its birth and upbringing. Dr. Francis Ramaley's zoological wisdom added an important element to the plan: he picked for the cabin a "mosquito-free site."

Logs, slabbed at a sawmill in Peaceful Valley, went by truck to Brainard Lake and by horse-drawn wagon to the cabin site. Joe Stapp built it and finished it in 1928. The Club paid the Forest Service an annual fee of twenty dollars.

The 1973 Altissimo concert. *Photo by Richard A. Jones.*

Waxing skis at the Arestua cabin, 1981. Betsy Caplan, Louise Bradley, Catherine Farrell. *Photo from Boulder CMC Archives.*

Boulder has used the Brainard cabin extensively, and it forms a center for Group activities. Today the Group keeps it open to the public on winter weekends, with volunteer hosts who, says Ann Hayes, "must know how to tap the icy flow of Mitchell Creek in the heart of winter" in order to serve, for fifty cents or a dollar, unlimited amounts of hot tea and instant coffee (cocoa costs too much). A manual for hosts, *The Brainard Bible,* co-authored by Stan and Margaret Huntting, explains the idiosyncrasies of the cabin's stoves, lights, locks, latches, and more. It is meant to be read with concentration and followed assiduously.

Boulder has cut three ski trails into the cabin, which has recovered its status (a status lost during the war due to non-use and mouse nests made from the mattress stuffing) as a center for the Boulder Group.

Cabin enthusiasts in Boulder built more cabins. The Pfiffner Hut, near East Portal, had a vibrant life beginning in 1967. Ann Hayes says that high snowfall often totally buried the hut structure. "To locate the hibernating hut, a skier who had just mounted the steep, twisting trail would scan the horizon for a stove pipe sticking out of an otherwise

Wilderness Kids snowshoe hikers Marcia, Danny, Michelle, Jamie, and Eddy Hunter on return from First Creek cabin, May 30, 1982. *Photo by Bill Hunter.*

innocent-looking drift. Digging out the Pfiffner was part of the ritual of entry." Designed for low maintenance, it wasn't; snow creep weakened it and the Group dismantled it in 1986.

Bob Kamper and Hugh McCaffrey organized Altissimo concerts at the hut: musicians (twenty-seven at the first concert in 1971) with violins, cellos, basses, woodwinds, and horns trudged the four miles to the hut to present breathtaking concerts. Three hundred concert-goers climbed the trail for the 1977 concert. Because of the environmental impact of such a crowd, Altissimo never performed again.

Jofrid Sodal designed Boulder's third cabin, Arestua, dedicated in 1970. He modeled it after its Norwegian namesake, "hearthfire hut." Located above Lake Eldora ski area on Guinn Mountain, it sleeps twelve on padded benches for ski tours around East Portal or over Rollins Pass to Winter Park.

Other groups have cabins, too. Denver has had First Creek, on the west side of Berthoud Pass, since 1933. The Forest Service built it of logs, well chinked and insulated, for $200 in materials and $750 of CCC labor. CMC (Denver) has always handled reservations. Now each fall CMC cabin work parties stock it with wood and clean it up for the forthcoming season. Denver also has had an interest in a series of other backcountry "lodges" like the West Portal, Pennsylvania Mine, and Mayflower Gulch huts. Only the First Creek cabin has survived the test of time.

Jim and Jessie Kunkle, in 1953, gave Pikes Peak a cabin near St.

Peters Dome, accessible from the Gold Camp Road and a half mile of "a somewhat dubious access road . . . in summer." The Group used it for many social activities like potluck suppers. But it proved expensive to maintain, and a frequent target for vandals. In 1958, Jacobs and Koerner report that "a disquieted group of mountaineers made a last trek to the cabin to hold a demolition party and King Kunkle's Kastle was dynamited out of existence."

WINTER SPORTS

The Club had an intense involvement in the evolution of skiing in Colorado — both backcountry and downhill. At first, of course, it was

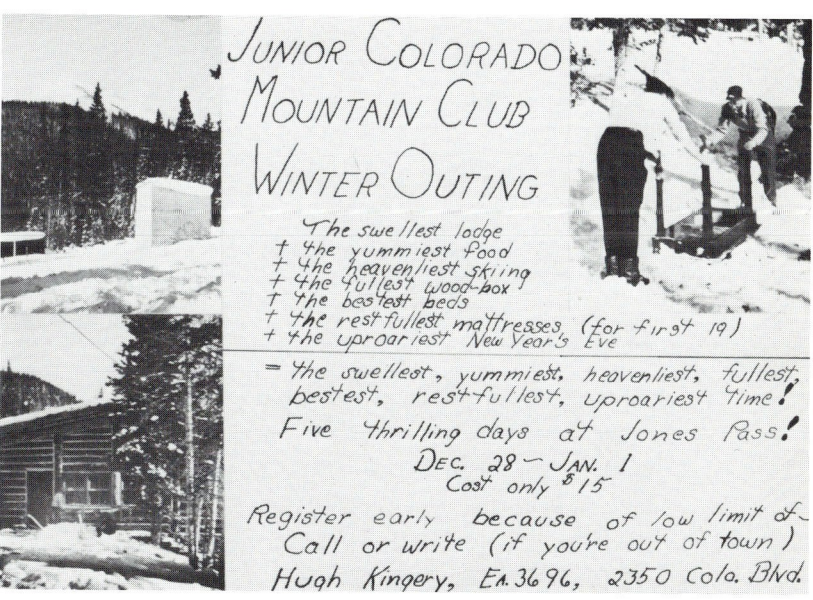

The Juniors announced their 1949 outing with a picture post card. The lodge at Jones Pass entertained them for several winter outings. In 1941, the Juniors' *T&T* reporter described the trip. One night "the girls found their sleeping bags with zippers sewed to the bottoms of the bags, rucksacks emptied, etc. A small party of boys slept in a cabin a mile above, however, just for safety's sake." *Photo from CMC Archives.*

Skiers on the Club's February 2-11 trip to Hot Sulphur Springs. *Photo from CMC Archives.*

all backcountry. The Club had those remarkable outings to Fern Lake and Fort Collins had Chambers Lake.

It also took many ski trips to Rilliet Hill, located on Lookout Mountain. Here skiers trekked up and skied down to learn and to perfect their telemarking techniques, assiduously avoiding the barbed-wire fence which stretched across the bottom of the slope.

Early Colorado skiing differed considerably from the 1988 version. Henry Buchtel described the situation in a 1939 *T&T* article.

"We all had our special secret formulas for ski wax. As I recall, mine was six parts paraffin to four parts beeswax with one drop of oil of coriander and a dash of paprika. (I may have confused this with my gin recipe but no matter: the wax was no good anyway.) This was melted on the stove, thoroughly mixed and poured into jelly glasses to harden. We ironed it onto the ski. It wouldn't slide downhill, nor would it stick enough to allow climbing. In wet snow each ski weighed so much that the muscles so hypertrophied have never atrophied.

"The same formula with the addition of two parts of linseed oil, one part of whale oil, and a lemon rind was used for shoe grease.

"In November 1923 our fool's paradise was interrupted by the advent of Lt. N. Delgi 'Bend more the knee' Albizzi. Before trusting himself to take us out skiing he talked to us at Agnes Vaille's. We had a terrible argument about his idea that one should ski with bent knees. Everyone knew that the proper way to ski was with the body bent forward and the knees stiff. He also rudely awakened us by making us take cross country trips, climb uphill on our skis, and other daring innovations, such as attempting to turn.

Opposite Page: Club ski trip, circa 1917. *Photo from CMC Archives.*

Many a CMCer learned to ski on Rilliet Hill. *Photo from CMC Archives.*

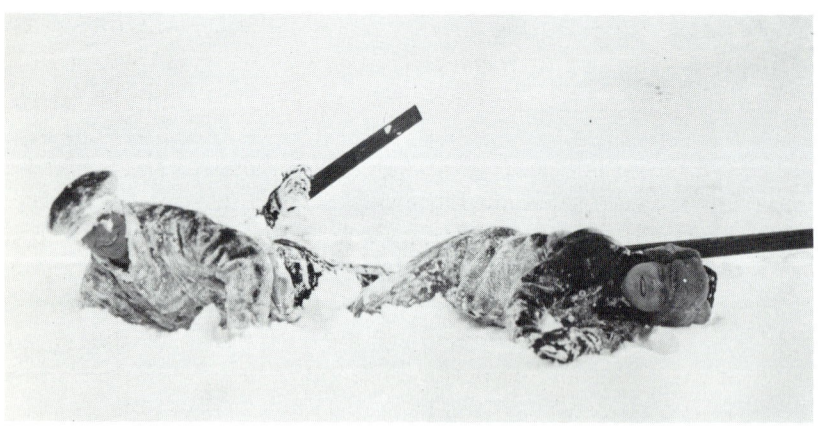

Or tried to learn to ski — George Barnard and Miss Croasdale. *Photo from CMC Archives.*

"We were introduced to a real torture device, the Albizzi harness. This was a long thin leather strap wound around the foot in an intricate pattern so that circulation was immediately suppressed, and I believe permanently impaired. . . . Those of you who did not experience skiing both before and after Albizzi cannot imagine how he revolutionized

Colorado skiing. We had been used to sliding down hill in a track and then carrying our skis back (a great advance was made by the genius who bored holes in the tips, and pulled the skis by a cord tied around the waist). Albizzi made us ski in soft snow . . . made us practice turning and stopping otherwise than sitz marking. His skiing position was exactly that used today by the very expert [in 1939]."

The new skiing technique launched by Albizzi, says Jan Robertson, "avalanched through the CMC so that it seemed to have become exclusively a skiing club. . . . An article in T&T translated from German described Hannes Schneider's Arlberg technique. The article sounded very modern until one examined the accompanying photographs closely and realized that the skiers' heels were raised."

A Fort Collins ski climb from the Group's Chambers Lake cabin provided entertainment for years afterward. The goal was the saddle between Clark and Cameron peaks. Laura Makepeace reported, "The climb became steeper and steeper while the snow became harder and harder. Then the inevitble happened — a ski slipped on the hard crust. Down slid one of the invincibles (only the men attempted it), faster and faster on five points instead of two. Then he began to disintegrate — one pole flew in one direction the other in another. The watchers saw two pairs of glasses fly through the air; a camera, knapsack, extra coat, and other articles of clothing were strewn over the mountainside. They began to wonder how soon parts of the skier himself would be decorating the landscape, but fortunately he came to rest in one piece. By the time he had collected all of his impedimenta it was time to start down the trail if the skiers were to reach the cabin with light enough to see the way."

T&T discussed ski techniques in the thirties. CMC discovered superb skiing at West Portal and on Berthoud Pass. Without ski tows, the Club ran a ski bus on Berthoud Pass in the 1935 to 1937 seasons as a ski lift for downhill-minded skiers. For a time the Club sponsored sanctioned ski races — club team races in 1938-1939, a regular downhill in 1941, and Junior races from 1947 to 1952.

Gradually the Club returned to backcountry skiing. In the late forties, the Club conducted ski climbs with many leaders from veterans of the Tenth Mountain Division. Skiers used wooden army surplus skis and strapped "climbing skins" to ski bottoms for uphill climbing. For downhill runs they wrapped the skins around their waists or stuffed them in their packs and they enjoyed real backcountry powder skiing on

In 1954, Club skiers used downhill skis with climbing skins attached. Here, Western Slopers Harry Harris, Bill Rossi, and Jeff Greer prepare for an uphill slog and a downhill thrill in front of Taggert Hut, Montezuma Basin, near Aspen, April 3, 1954. *Photo by Bob Beverly.*

downhill skis.

This equipment gave way to the skinny skis favored by Olympic racers and nordic natives. Legions of people have discovered the sport, and now the club schedules over 100 ski touring trips each winter.

Pikes Peakers started in the 1960s going to Steamboat Springs for expert instruction, and by 1970 began their own ski touring clinic. "The monotonous step turn," said Jacobs and Koerner, "began to take a backseat to the graceful telemark which had gone into hibernation since the Depression." (That reference to "graceful" proves they haven't seen the movies of the 1920s CMC in action.) A telemark clinic which

Opposite Page: Ski climbers head for Pearl Basin, March 1963. (Mike and Fred Ruckhaus.) *Photo by Gwen Toepfer.*

taught "the complex sequence of movements necessary to complete the difficult turn" sent participants "to various hot tubberies . . . trying to soak out their temporary lameness, only to find them back at the slopes next weekend in typical mountaineering spirit practicing technique and obtaining new wounds."

With the revival of ski touring came a revival of ski racing — in this case on skinny skis. The Boulder Group started it with races to the Pfiffner Hut in 1968 and later added the Gayle Waldrop, Alice Holubar, and Gold Spitoon races. One year an underdog won the Waldrop classic, writes Ann Hayes, when the hot-shots followed the trail of a recreational skier bound for Isabel Lake. "Myriam Friggens had the wits to stay on the true course around Long Lake . . . and won the trophy!"

The Gold Spitoon race benefited the CMC Huts and Trails Committee, and from its inaugural in 1974 involved contestants from other groups. In 1984, the trophy, the "battered and beloved spitoon, which had so admirably served for the communal swilling of champagne that followed every race, sprung a fatal leak. That year . . . racers . . . quaffed . . . bubbley fluid that gushed from a hole in the bottom."

Snowshoers, 1948.
Photo by Virginia Nolan.

Boulder members wax enthusiastic (even though many no longer wax their now-plastic skis) about the fun of these events. No longer held, they unfortunately became a victim of sky-rocketing insurance costs.

During the heyday of skis and skins, skiers had to know how to ski downhill, for if they went up, they had to go down. Many Club members preferred not to deal with that, so that for winter trips they opted for old-fashioned snowshoes. Snowshoeing has kept a steady pace compared with backcountry skiing, and many summer hikers have derived great satisfaction from that more sedate mode of winter transportation. Denver reporter Carolyn Campbell called them "tennis rackets *au pied*." The Denver snowshoe group sponsored an obstacle course race at Echo Lake in 1953; Jim MacMillan won, as he was the only contestant to complete the course without falling. Sometimes snowshoers share trips with the skiers — who go uphill more slowly and downhill more rapidly than the even-paced snowshoers.

TRAILS

Accessibility involves trails. The Club took its first trip along the Beaver Brook route on December 1, 1912. The trail itself, although it winds through Denver Mountain Parks land and municipal money built it, has existed since 1917 because of the persistence of CMC members, especially Club presidents Henry Brooks and George Barnard.

Other Club groups shared this interest in trail development. Fort Collins planned and built a nature trail on Mount McConnell. Led by Frank Goeder, the Club blazed the trail on November 4, 1930; construction began in May. Guided through "fresh and untrodden paths, rocky formations, fern-filled glades ideal for out-door nature study," the pick-axes and shovels cut down not a single tree. Labels, made of zinc, enameled in white, lettered with black India ink and waterproofed, explained nature's story.

Fort Collins also went to the aid of an old friend in 1977. The devastating Big Thompson flood of 1976 wiped out the trail up Fort

Opposite Page: Combination ski/snowshoe trip above Montgomery Dam, Mosquito Range. *Photo by Spencer Swanger.*

Collins' mountain mecca, Greyrock. Immediate response by Club members and the Forest Service resulted in scouting a new trail and building it. Club members built ten retaining walls, constructed a trailway across a flooded channel, and cut trail treads along hillsides. By April 1 the next year they had put the new trail in excellent condition, and the Club had donated $27,000 in work.

CMC co-sponsored a trail-building effort into Pierre Basin at the base of Capitol Peak in 1952. Bob Ormes reported that the new trail lacked a good bridge across Snowmass Creek, "thus the trail is what I was hoping for — a foot path which will not be loused up by excessive horse use, at least for a time."

The Club's Trail and Shelter Committee report in 1934 proposed that the Forest Service build "a continuous trail — within the timberline zone wherever possible — from Echo Lake on Mount Evans to Bear Lake in Rocky Mountain National Park." The August 1934 *T&T* has an elaborate map of the proposed trail, and also shows existing roads and trails in the area. Apparently the Forest Service lacked the money, and certainly the Mountain Club did.

The trail building movement burgeoned in the 1960s with the idea of a Continental Divide Trail. Club trips went to far reaches of the state to mark the route, generally over existing trails, with tin can lids painted baby blue. The minutes of the Pikes Peak Group report that trail markers

Indefatigable Gudy Gaskill.
Photo by Janet Robertson.

were usually "tuna fish cans, painted blue, . . . nailed to trees to mark the way. . . . Beer cans work much better, as they . . . serve a double purpose." Perhaps Pikes Peakers don't eat tuna.

Two binders in the Club library and articles in T&T describe the route of that trail, with pictures by the parties that marked it. However, the Club developed second thoughts about the trail. The Forest Service draft plan piloted hikers into overused areas, sensitive habitats, and archeological sites and it projected increased motorized use, with, CMC perceived, resultant environmental damage. This trail also would have attracted inexperienced hikers to high altitudes — timberline and above — without proper training and equipment. These problems led the CMC in 1982 to rescind its endorsement of a Continental Divide Trail.

As the Continental Divide Trail became quiescent, another trail idea became extremely active. Merrill Hastings, publisher of *Colorado Magazine,* proposed a "Colorado Trail." It would follow the southwest passage from Denver to Durango, "350 miles as the foot slogs," said Walter Jessel, reporting in T&T in 1974.

In the same year, CMC began its trail maintenance outings, the first one led by Vaughn Ham, Gudy Gaskill, and Hugh McCaffrey. Annual trips turned into trail-building trips.

Many Club members involved themselves in the planning and build-

Colorado Trail work: Tom Rockwell and Vito Tursi in action. *Photo courtesy of Gudy Gaskill.*

ing, but one immersed herself in the Colorado Trail — and that's why we have it. Gudy Gaskill, first woman president of CMC, has unbounded energy. She served on the Outings Committee and her gentle persistence saw many outings to successful culminations.

She invoked incredible effort to plan, and to build, the Colorado Trail. By the time of the trail's dedication in 1988, she involved not only every group of CMC but legions of other organizations — private and governmental — and people from all over the United States and several foreign countries.

All through the 1980s, summer schedules and *T&T* announced trail crew schedules — forty-six for 1987 which garnered 800 volunteers. Those trips succeed because they offer more than simply work, albeit rewarding work. On a typical 1979 trip the group worked and climbed on alternate days; they ascended Mounts Elbert and Massive and enjoyed a raft trip on the Arkansas.

The effort has beckoned trail builders from throughout the country and brought national recognition to Gudy. She deserves it — for if Fort Collins contributed $27,000 worth of work to Greyrock, work on the Colorado Trail is worth a million dollars.

OTHER ACCESS

Some hikers need help to enjoy the mountains. In 1970, the Denver Group started a sharing tradition: white cane hikes. They took blind hikers into the mountains and gave them the opportunity to experience the out-of-doors. With one sighted hiker per blind hiker, the trips proved immensely popular with the blind. Long-time Club member Wilbert Moehrke, whose sight, after an accident, became more and more impaired, prodded the Club into this activity. It succeeded so well that he received a presidential citation for his leadership.

The Club has access problems, too. Private landowners often control the approach routes to popular climbs. Culebra Peak, the best-known problem, now can be climbed only upon payment of a fee to the landowner, and only on Sundays, in July. After some years of ad hoc action, the Club included access problems in the job description of conservation coordinator Anne Vickery. Then in 1986 it set up an Access Committee. Targeted for action were Centennial Cone (completely

White Cane hike on Range View Trail, Flagstaff Mountain, May 24, 1970. *Photo by Elwyn Arps.*

blocked), the Cloyses Lake approach to Huron and Missouri, Como Lake near Blanca Peak, and Chair Mountain (where a locked gate on public land blocks access).

ROCK CLIMBING

As members of a "mountain club," the first climbers expended their energies attaining summits. This often involved arduous approaches to remote peaks, by train, pack horse, and the like. As they developed their skills, they began to use ropes, pitons, carabiners, and other accoutrements of technical climbing. The San Juan Mountaineers (Dave and Dwight Lavender, Mel Griffiths, and a few others) specialized in first ascents and first routes in the San Juans, and these often required technical techniques. In 1929, Steve Hart, Bill Ervin, and Carl Blaurock made the first climb of Lone Eagle. They had tried one time from the town of Ward on the Eastern Slope; this time they packed in by horse from Monarch Lake. They climbed to the ridge, traversed it, sometimes hanging a leg on either side, and finally followed a short chimney to the top. The hard part wasn't the climbing — it was getting there in the first place.

Albert Ellingwood made high peak technical climbs not only in the

Crestones, but also throughout southern Colorado. Bob Ormes, who learned from Ellingwood, pioneered routes in the Garden of the Gods and the northeast face of Blanca. Ormes ranked the north face of Lone Eagle among the very best in the state in a *T&T* article in which he described a climb on the 1940 outing.

The Flatirons beckoned to Boulder climbers like Rudy Johnson (subsequently author of the billboard bill in the state legislature) and Everett Long (who finished his first climb barefoot after rain rendered his tennis shoes too slick to stick).

T&T reported on many first ascents during the thirties: Shark Tooth, west face of Capitol, north face of Crestone Peak, the Index, Rock of Ages in the Tetons, the Wham Ridge on Vestal Peak. Roy Murchison and Bob Ormes claimed a first ascent of Chimney Rock, northwest of Fort Collins; they disclaimed a previous attempt because the climber had drilled twelve holes in the rock and inserted iron pegs — "this to gain 35 feet in elevation."

Originally technical climbing techniques aided a climber in getting to the top of a mountain, maybe the only way, maybe the harder way. The Lone Eagle climbers used them for that ascent. Ellingwood used them on the climbs he pioneered on Crestone Needle with Eleanor Davis and Eleanor Bartlett and on La Plata Mountain — routes which now bear his name. They were aids, though, not stepping stones. Mel Griffiths of the San Juan Mountaineers, agreeing with Ormes and Murchison, put it this way:

"In general it may be said that any peak, the summit of which has been attained solely through the use of spikes for hand and foot holds, has not been climbed; it has been ravished."

While these climbers belonged to the CMC, most of the climbs were not official Club activities. The development of technical climbing, especially in the past twenty years, has not involved the CMC as a group.

The character of technical climbing has indeed changed: rock climbing for the sake of rock climbing; uses of hardware unimagined a few years ago (both the uses and the hardware). Modern enthusiasts climb boulders and pinnacles; they eschew the high peaks, partly because it

Opposite Page: Steve Hart (later president of the Colorado Historical Society) and Bill Ervin straddle the ridge on the first ascent of Lone Eagle, Labor Day 1929. *Photo by Carl Blaurock.*

takes so much time and effort to get to them and to the technical challenges which they offer. Modern climbers can attack a spire in Boulder Canyon in an afternoon, but it takes days and time-consuming logistics to mount an assault on the east face of Longs or Wham Ridge on Vestal Peak.

On the other hand, the Club does sponsor numerous schools to introduce Club members to the rudiments of technical climbing. Knowledge of the fundamentals of rock climbing still has an importance to high peak climbers; they often use these fundamentals (equipment and techniques) on their climbs.

THE PEOPLE

Of course the passion for hiking and climbing which CMC members develop through the Club extends beyond Club trips. Members become proficient mountaineers through the Colorado Mountain Club, and practice their passion on private trips as well. First to climb all the Fourteeners, in 1923, were Carl Blaurock and Bill Ervin. Albert Ellingwood did it next, and Mary Cronin became the fourth, and first woman, to climb them all, in 1934. (Mary Cronin's first CMC contact came with a "Mystery Trip" in 1921, on the Beaver Brook Trail. Her last, from her home in Seattle via the U.S. mail, a 1975 contribution of $100 to help retire the clubroom mortgage.) Jim Gehres has climbed them all — eight times. In December 1987, the Club listed 389 climbers who had reached the summits of all Colorado's 14,000-foot peaks.

Lots of people set records — all the Fourteeners, the 100 highest, all the named Front Range summits, etc. But the more important records belong to those who volunteer for jobs with this "highly individual corporation." CMC founder Rogers' custom of volunteerism has lots of adherents — they keep the Club going. Club presidents, group chairmen, *T&T* staff, groundskeepers, equipment chairmen, hut committees — the people who take these jobs really set the important records — and mostly unsung ones.

Vaughn Ham is the only person to serve as CMC president, Group chairman, *and T&T* editor. Alex Carson, proofreader extraordinaire and expert on mountaineering language, has a different distinction: he has served on the *T&T* staff longer than anyone — thirty-seven years and

Climbers from a Club outing on the summit of Longs Peak, 14,256 feet, at sunrise, August 1913. *Photo from CMC Archives.*

still going — and outlasted twenty-one editors.

The most admired people in the Club are the good leaders. Old-timers speak with admiration of the two best: George Harvey and Bill Ervin. Since then the Club has had many fine leaders, too many to name. Good leaders make good trips; good leaders form the backbone of the Colorado Mountain Club.

Epilogue

The Colorado Mountain Club has enjoyed seventy-five vigorous years. How will it continue its highly individual relationship with the mountains and with Coloradoans? CMC's 1988 President Gary Grange offers these thoughts.

"The past seventy-five years have clearly demonstrated the remarkable force that dedicated volunteers can generate. They have devoted hours and even years to goals which have benefited all lovers of the Colorado mountains and outdoors, not just CMC members.

"Speaking pragmatically, I would predict external influences as much as internal decisions will dictate how the Club will plan and conduct its activities: for example, concerns over liability of the Club, its leaders, and volunteers; reactions to increasing regulation over access and use of public lands.

"The Club will attract more members and more groups. New members will seek training and education in mountain recreation and safety. Administering the affairs of the Groups and the Club will most likely rely more on paid professionals than on volunteers.

"Our volunteer heritage will carry us through the next seventy-five years, inspired by the irresistible lure of the Colorado mountains and led by dedicated outdoorsmen and environmentalists who commit their time and energies to supporting this wonderful organization."

The CMC will no doubt persist as a highly individual Club devoted to a highly individual place, the Colorado Rockies.

Opposite Page: Bill Ervin and Carl Blaurock achieved the first ascent of Lone Eagle Peak in 1929. *Photo from CMC Archives.*

Special Articles

The following list of articles from *Trail & Timberline* is offered to whet the appetites of readers who would like to learn more about the history of the Colorado Mountain Club.

COLORADO MOUNTAIN CLUB

"The CMC — Its First Ten Years," by Lucretia Vaile *et al.* Special Anniversary Issue, April 1922.

"Fifty Golden Years of Colorado Mountaineering." Special Anniversary Issue, April 1962.

"CMC Recruit," by Jean Waterhouse. April 1950: 56. A new CMC member shanghaied — instead of a nature hike, a winter climb from Loveland Pass.

"Non-Leader Finds No Peak," by Vaughn Ham. July 1957: 99. A humorous essay on leadership.

"Seventy Pounds of Raw Carrots," by Margaret L. Mattoon. November 1952: 163. Reminiscences of an outing cook.

"First Climb," by Janet Chatin. August 1958: 105. A climb of West Spanish Peak.

"Never Summer Backpack," by Esther Holt. January 1952: 9.

"Snowshoe Trip in Knee-Deep Water," by Martha Williams. August 1962: 137.

"A Plane Trip Around the 14,000 Foot Peaks," by H.B. Van Valkenburgh III. September 1951: 110.

MOUNTAINEERING

"The Eastern Arete of the Crestone Needle," by Albert R. Ellingwood. November 1925: 6. First ascent of "Ellingwood Arete."

"Climb of Mount Lindbergh," by Carl Blaurock. November 1929: 10. First ascent of the mountain now named Lone Eagle.

Opposite Page: The Flatirons. *Photo by John Loren.*

"The 'Tooth' and Its Companions," by Hugh W. Hetherington. July 1942: 91. An early climb of El Diente.

"The Conquest of Banner," by Robert E. More. September 1950: 131. A major ascent of 1,200 feet, with descent by the new technique, suspendersitz rappel.

"The Second Conquest of Banner," by William E. Davis. September 1961: 162. Dramatic description of a heroic climb.

"Exploring the Mount Zirkel-Dome Peak Wild Area," by Margaret Chase. August 1957: 111. A trail and climbing guide.

"Wilderness Adventure," by Rich Griffith. August 1950: 118. Near disaster at Disaster Falls, Green River, Dinosaur National Monument.

"Struck by Lightning," by Nelson Chenkin and Judith Friend. September 1980: 154. CPR first aid taken with CMC allowed him to save his wife's life.

"Thoughts from a Litter," by David H. Tripp. October 1962: 161. Victim describes a climbing accident.

"Philosophy of Mountaineering," by Joseph Bosetti. February 1937: 22.

"Philosophy of Mountaineering," by Dave Gaskill. September 1949: 127.

"Why Climb?" April 1926: 60. Articles from masculine and feminine viewpoints.

SKIING

"Skiing B.E.P.," by Henry Buchtel. January 1939: 5. Allegedly a historical account of early skiing in Colorado but actually a hilarious report on the vagaries of early skiing.

"When Skiers Were a Curiosity," by Marjorie Perry. January 1950: 7. Skiers, touring on a railroad track, meet a rotary snowplow on a trestle.

COLORADO MOUNTAIN HISTORY

"The Mystic Huajatolla," by Frances P. Evans. July 1941. History and legends of the Spanish Peaks.

"Ascent of Grays Peak," March 1955. Condensation of an article in an 1872 issue of *Scribner's Magazine*.

"Princeton Boys in the Rockies," by Louisa Ward Arps. July 1942. A history of early climbing in the Sawatch.

"Pittsburgh on the Slate," by Louisa Ward Arps. June 1956: 87. History of the West Elks area, keyed to a forthcoming outing.

SCIENCE AND LITERATURE

"Hazards of Mountain Writing," by Robert M. Ormes. July 1961: 126. Discusses bloopers by Ormes and others.

"Lt. Carpenter's Grasshopper," by Gordon Alexander. July 1962: 109. A sidelight of the first climb of Mount of the Holy Cross — a flightless grasshopper collected on that climb and never found since.

"Water Ouzels of Our Mountain Streams," by Ferd Kleinschnitz. February 1948: 39.

"Are Our Glaciers Disappearing?" by Ronald L. Ives. January 1936: 3.

NON-COLORADO MOUNTAINEERING

"Shiprock Finale," by Ralph Bedayan. February 1940. First ascent of Shiprock.

"Seventeen-and-a-Half," by David Lavender. November 1950: 159. The longest mile, found on the CMC Wind River outing.

"We Walked the Rainbow Trail," by Paul and Ruth Gorham. March 1951: 30. A three-day trek to Rainbow Bridge.

"The Beckoning Rainbow," by Ruth Kuenning. May 1952: 84. A two-day trek to Rainbow Bridge.

"The Climb of Mount Rainier," by Allen Auten. December 1954: 169.

"Climbs in the Northern St. Elias Mountains," by William E. Davis. January 1958: 3. Two expeditions to the Canadian Rockies and five first ascents.

"Mount St. Helens: The Fujiyama of America," by Dwight Hamilton. March 1956: 39. Climbing St. Helens before it erupted.

"Canterbury Pilgrimage," by Virginia Copeland. April 1953: 53. A brief trip to Canterbury.

"Kilimanjaro and the Mountains of the Moon," by Winona Campbell. September 1957: 127. A seventeen page account of a major Club expedition to Africa.

Index

A

A Guide to the Geology of the Boulder Region, 51
Albizzi, N. Delgi, 104, 106-107
Allen, Russ, 61-62
American Flats, 15-16
Arapaho Peaks, 36
Arndt, Karl, 91
Arnold, Bill, 41, 87
Arps, Elwyn, 25, 30, 31, 53
Arps, Lousia Ward, 25, 31, 53-56, 97
Aspen Group, 42
Aspen Mountain Rescue, 42
Auten, Al, 80, 93
Avalanche awareness, 60

B

Bailey, Rusty, 62
Bannister, Ward, 76
Barbee, Bob, 55
Barnard, George C., 13, 15, 23, 25, 28, 106, 111
Bartlett, Eleanor, 32, 116
Barton, Harlan, 53
Beaver Brook Trail, 28
Berman, Mike, 38
Berthoud Pass, 107
Bethel, Ellsworth, 22, 27, 55
Beverly, Bob, 39, 53
Bishop, Barry, 93
Blanca Peak, 55, 64
Blaurock, Carl, 51, 86, 115, 117
Boucher, Stan, 22, 41, 87
Bouck, Harriett Vaille, 55-56
Bouck, Polly, 15
Boulder Group, 29-30, 34-37, 51, 54, 59, 100, 102
"Boulder Mountain Park Trail Map," 53
Bowles, Mary Hitch, 38
Bradley, Rick, 80
Brainard Lake, 53
Brainard Lake cabin, 37, 48, 100-101
Braun, Fred, 42
Brewer, William, 54
Brooks, Henry, 27, 111
Brown, Mrs. Junius F., 45
Buchtel, Henry, 51, 91, 104
Bucknam, Dave, 37, 38
Burns, Robert, 35
Burrage, Severance, 36

C

Cameron Pass, 37
Campbell, Carolyn, 85, 111
Capitol Peak, 66, 112
Carson, Alex, 76, 118
Carter, Freddy, 42
Castle, Peak, 39
Challenger Point, 55-56
Chambers Lake, 99, 107
Chatin, Janet, 41, 86
Chenkin, Jude, 61
Chenkin, Nelson, 61
Cheyenne Mountain High School, 29
Cheyenne Mountaineers, 33
Chicago Basin, 89-90
Collier, Malcolm, 91
Colorado Mountain Club, organization, 22-23; membership statistics, 25; trip classifications, 31; groups, 31-45; secretaries, 45-48; clubrooms, 49; publications, 50-55; peak nomenclature, 55-56; mountaineering schools, 58-63; library 67, 69; conservation efforts, 71-83; outings, 87-99; cabins, 99-103; winter activities, 103-111
Colorado Mountain Club Foundation, 48, 54
Colorado Open Space Council, 80
Colorado Trail, 113-114
Court House Mountain, 16
Cowles, George, 44
Cowles, Wanda, 44
Coxcomb, 16
Craig Creek, 30
Crisp, Katherine Bruderlin, 45-46
Cronin, Dan, 60
Cronin, Mary, 25, 91, 118
Culebra Peak, 45, 114
Curtis, Gladys, 30, 35
Curtis, Harry, 35

D

Darby, Lorena, 40, 63
Davis, Bill, 38
Davis, C. Earl, 87
Davis, Eleanor, 32, 116
Denver Group, 30-33, 59, 65
Denver Wilderness Kids, 43-44, 102

E

Eagle Peak, 42
Eagles Nest Wilderness Area, 79
Echo Park Dam, 77
Elbert, Mount, 29, 38, 53
El Diente Peak, 52
Ellingwood, Albert, 115-116, 118
Ellis, A. G., 34
El Pueblo Group, 41-42, 60
Engineer Mountain, 15
Enos Mills Group, 44, 80
Eppich, Elinor, 46
Ervin, Bill, 115, 117-119
Euser, Barbara, 49
Evans, Mount, 25, 89

F

Fern Lake Lodge, 82, 96-99
Field, Harry, 75
First Creek Cabin, 102

Floyd, Margaret, 33
Fort Collins Group, 28, 51, 61, 71, 75, 107, 111
Foster, Frankie, 50
Foster, Mike, 49, 54, 60
Fourteen Thousand Feet, 53
Fourteeners, 25, 46, 53, 66, 118
Francisco, Ethel, 86
Friends of Colorado, 45
Front Range Club, 34
"Front Range Panorama," 53
Frost, Tad, 38
Fuehrer, Roger, 78

G

Gaskill, Gudy, 112-114
Gehres, Jim, 118
Genesee Mountain Park, 72
Gilpin Lake, 8
Glacier National Park, 86
Glasier, Lloyd, 65
Glenwood Group, 45
Goeder, Frank, 111
Grand Canyon dams, 79-80
Grange, Gary, 121
Grays Peak, 25, 37, 67-68
Green, Pansy, 33
Greene, Lenore, 68
Greer, Jeff, 108
Griffiths, Mel, 115-116
Guadagno, Dick, 78
Guide to the Colorado Mountains, 51

H

Hagerman, Percy, 54
Hallum, Gus, 42
Ham, Vaughn, 113, 118
Harris, Harry, 39, 108
Hart, Jerry, 53
Hart, Steve, 115, 117
Harvey, George, 45
Harvey, Grace, 46
Hastings, Merrill, 113
Hayes, Ann, 35, 101, 109
Hendrie, Edna, 55-56
Henson Creek, 15
High Country Names, 54-55
Holt, Esther, 53
Holubar, Alice, 109
Holubar, Roy, 60
Holy Cross Wilderness, 82
Homestake II, 82
Hondius, Piet, 60
Hornbein, Tom, 61
Huerfano Group, 41
Hunt, Everett, 59
Hunter, Bill, 43
Huntting, Margaret, 101
Huntting, Stan, 101
Huron Peak, 52
Hutchison, Charles, 100

J

Jacobs, Randy, 33
Jackson, Edward, 32
Jackson, William Henry, 65
Johnson, Dale, 95

Johnson, Rudolph, 75, 116
Johnson, Yvonne, 41
Junior Group, 29, 37-38

K

Kamper, Bob, 22, 102
Kaub, Cedric, 31-32, 47, 76
Kaye, Steve, 63
Kelley, Clint, 61
Kelly, George, 38
Kendall, Claribel, 35
Kendall, Florence, 35
Kennon, Anne Byrd, 47
Kiley, Enda, 48
Kingery, Elinor Eppich, 15, 46, 53-54, 93, 97
Kingery, Hugh M., 36, 99
Koerner, Jane, 33
Kruetzer, Billy, 55-56
Kunkle, Jim and Jessie, 102

L

Lake Eldora, 102
Lamm, Dick, 79, 94
Lamm, Dottie, 79
Lavender, David, 115
Lavender, Dwight, 115
Leopold, Estella, 80
Lindsey, Malcolm, 38, 55
Lindsey, Mount, 56-57
Little Bear Peak, 25
Lone Eagle Peak, 115
Long, Everett, 22, 116
"Longmont's Mountain Skyline," 53
Longs Peak, 13, 40, 84-85
Longs Peak Group, 39-41, 53, 63
Los Alamos Mountaineers, 45

M

MacMillan, Jim, 111
Makepeace, Laura, 71, 107
Manard, Alice, 46
McCaffrey, Hugh, 102, 113
McConnell, Mount, Nature Trail, 28, 51, 111
McCorkle, John, 60
Moehrke, Wilbert, 114
Mohling, Franz, 22, 60
Morgan, Aurel, 53
Mountain oriented first aid, (MOFA), 60-61
Mountain Wildlife of Northern Colorado, 51
Mills, Enos, 48
Missouri Mountain, 53
Mullen, Al, 93
Murch, Helen, 35
Murchison, Roy, 25, 116
Myatt, Billy, 89, 91

N

Needle Mountains, 31, 91
Never Summer Range, 89
North Maroon Peak, 26
Notes on Mountaineering in the Elk Mountains, 54

O

Ormes, Bob, 51, 112, 116
Ouray, 14

P

Palmer, Russ, 40, 53
Paproski, Irene, 29
Partridge, Betsy Cowles, 51
Penland, Floyd, 33
Penland, William, 33
Peterson, Marian, 48
Peterson, Marilyn, 48
Pfiffner Hut, 101, 109
Pierce, Trudy, 53
Pikes Peak, 13
Pikes Peak Group, 29, 32-34, 60, 66, 75, 80, 112
Pikes Peak Mountain Club, 34
Porzak, Glenn, 96
Poughkeepsie Gulch, 14
Pownall, Dick, 93

Q

Quandary Peak, 42

R

Ramaley, Bill, 75
Ramaley, Francis, 100
Red Mountain, 14
Reese, Irene, 99
Richards, Sally, 48, 69
Richtofen, Mount, 10
Rilliet Hill, 104, 106
Robertson, Janet, 35, 48, 54, 100, 107
Rockwell, Robert, 44
Rockwell, Tom, 113
Rocky Mountain National Park, 54-55, 71, 75, 81
Rogers, Edmund, 55, 76-77
Rogers, James Grafton, 22, 24-25, 27, 118
Ross, Sally, 27
Rossi, Bill, 108
Runnette, Evelyn, 46-47, 65

S

Sabin, Florence, 22
Sabin, Mary, 22, 25, 27, 45
San Juan Group, 42
San Juan Mountaineers, 115
San Juan Outing, 1920, 88-89
Saum, Bud, 27
Schnackenberg, Jane, 93
Schnackenberg, Rudy, 60
Schnackenberg, Werner, 60
Sentinel Point, 32
Settles, Ella Jane, 47
Settles, Jean, 37
Shafroth, Morrison, 71
Shaw, Lloyd, 33
Sherman, Mount, 25, 41
Shirer, Mary, 33-34, 85
Silverstein, Alan, 49
Silverton, 14
Smedley, Will P., 13, 16, 18
Smith, C. Henry, 35
Smith, Daphne, 35
Snow, Georgia, 35
Sodal, Jofrid, 102
Sopris, Mount, 39

South Boulder Peak, 25, 28
Spreng, Fred, 91
Spreng, Mary, 91
Staehle, Henry, 52
Standley, Harry, 32, 64, 66
Stapp, Joe, 100
Stewart, Paul, 41-42
Stiles-Wainwright, Helen, 67
Strang, Hubert, 32
Stratton, Doris, 35
Summit Lake, 25
Summits to Reach, 49
Swallow, Alan, 51-52
Swanger, Spencer, 91
Sugarloaf, 83

T

Taggert Hut, 108
Taussig, Anna, 42
Texas Creek, 87
The Front Rangers, 54
Thompson, Frank E. "Pop", 35
Thompson, Peg, 35
Toll, Oliver, 55-56
Toll, Roger, 53, 55
Torreys Peak, 25, 67
Trail and Timberline, 25, 33, 51, 54, 66
Turner, Jim, 33
Turner, Pearl, 32
Tursi, Vito, 113

U

Uncompahgre Peak, 13, 16, 17, 19
Utter, Clyde, 13
Utter, Dr. (Rev.) David, 13, 18-19

V

Vaile, Howard, 91
Vaile, Lucretia, 21-22, 27
Vaille, Agnes, 46, 104
Vaille, Sally, 97
Van Valkenburg, Prof., 100
Vickery, Anne, 81, 114

W

Wagner, Julia, 33
Waldrop, Gayle, 100, 109
Walton, Harold, 96
Ward, Edith, 53
Ward, Orlando, 53
Weld County Group, 45
Wernette, Neil, 29
West Elk Group, 45
Western Slope Group, 39
Wetterhorn, 16-17, 20
Wheeler Peak, 42
Wildflowers of Northern Colorado, 51
Wilks, Sara E., 33
Wilson, Mount, 52, 55
Wilson Peak, 12
Wolcott, John, 37
Wright, Ken, 22, 25
Wright, Ruth, 22